Praise for
MAXIMIZING ORGANIZATIONAL PERFORMANCE

"I had the pleasure to browse this very interesting book from Dr. Patrick Behar-Courtois, *Maximizing Organizational Performance: A Guide to Effective Performance Coaching*.
What struck me is how the analysis and recommendations in this guide are so accurate to reality and our day-to-day group and hotel operations. The writer faithfully presents the importance of personal coaching in order to build high-performing and motivated individuals and teams.

I highly recommend this guidebook to any managers who wish to develop effective, tailor-made coaching programs and strong, winning teams of highly qualified individuals!"

—Vincent Lelay, vice president of operations at Accor Ambassador Korea

"Written in a highly engaging style, *Maximizing Organizational Performance* is a comprehensive treatise on an indispensable element of success: effective performance coaching. Dr. Behar-Courtois provides readers practical guidance on the many issues and methods of effective performance coaching. Users of this masterfully organized and thoroughly thought-out work will benefit greatly as they apply its wisdom to help others improve their effectiveness and derive greater satisfaction in what they do."

—Charles E. Watson, author of *Frontline Management Excellence*

"This book is a beautiful symphony of insight and practicality—a must-read for anyone who wants to understand why performance coaching is not just important, but essential to building competitive, resilient, and human-centered organizations. Dr. Patrick Behar-Courtois brings the rare depth of a seasoned strategist and the sensitivity of an experienced coach. With clarity and precision, he reveals how to unlock human potential in ways that are both profoundly practical and deeply human. His approach resonates like a well-conducted orchestra—each element purposeful, each insight empowering."

—Virak Chhuor, CEO and founder of Orchestral Insight

"*Maximizing Organizational Performance: A Guide to Effective Performance Coaching* by Patrick Behar-Courtois offers a fresh, practical approach to performance coaching, making it an essential read for executives. The book's holistic perspective on fostering a culture of continuous improvement is both innovative and actionable. With real-world examples and a focus on leadership and team dynamics, it provides valuable insights for driving organizational success. Executives will find it a useful resource for enhancing performance and aligning coaching strategies with their organization's unique needs."

—Sebastien Gauchet, managing director of Gerflor Asia

"A well-packed articulation of corporate anecdotes relatable to a plethora of organization performance issues. Dr. Behar-Courtois brings the reader right into the corporate battlefield and equips the professional with coaching frameworks and tools. A book with enlightening perspectives and an intrinsic call to action."

—Brian Sun, assistant director of executive career development at INSEAD business school

"Patrick was my coach a few years ago, and after reading his book, I immediately recognized the same common sense and pragmatism in the tools he describes. Over a decade later, I'm still using many of them—like SMART goals, 360-degree feedback, and competency assessments—with fantastic results. Recently, I discovered the Eisenhower Matrix through his book, and it's already transforming how my team prioritizes tasks, delivering impressive outcomes. This book is truly a powerhouse of efficiency for any organization!"

—Joel Dumont, sourcing and operations director at GiFi

"Thanks to his vast professional experience combined with his solid academic background, Dr. Behar-Courtois succeeds in seamlessly interweaving a 'get-on-to-work' approach to effective performance coaching with important theoretical concepts grounded in solid peer-reviewed research. This combination results in a thorough step-by-step guide, full of examples and a complete tool kit for immediate deployment, which is useful far beyond the coaching profession: top and middle managers, HR professionals, project managers, and team leaders can all benefit from this hands-on method to unleash performance gains out of their existing resources."

—Nuno Guimaraes da Costa, associate dean for research and impact at the Excelia Business School, associate editor for the *Business and Society Review*

"I have known Dr. Patrick Behar-Courtois since 2010, when I began my career in recruitment consultancy.

In today's competitive talent landscape, hiring the right people is a crucial first step, yet it is only the beginning.

Patrick's book offers a comprehensive guide to the next phase: building a talent-development cycle through effective performance coaching. Having navigated every role in the performance coaching process—from a frontline corporate worker to a coached individual, manager, and now a performance coach with a strong academic foundation—Patrick brings a multifaceted perspective, sharing practical insights and strategies. I am confident you will find his experienced feedback and advice essential as you prepare to win the talent battle!"

—Pierre-Yves Gerard, senior partner at CGL Consulting

"This book provided me with a clear road map for leveraging performance coaching to enhance employee engagement, leadership development, and overall productivity. It is packed with interesting real-world examples and practical tools. It provides guidance to leaders to foster a culture of continuous improvement that drives sustainable success in today's challenging business landscape."

—Philippe Angely, managing director of Virtuos, North Asia

"Dr. Patrick Behar-Courtois's *Maximizing Organizational Performance: A Guide to Effective Performance Coaching* is the game-changing tool kit needed by any leader looking to take their organization to the next level. Written in a relatable manner with personal insights and real-life case studies, this book provides a panoply of strategies to augment team effectiveness, with specific and actionable strategies to addressing modern challenges like remote work, employee retention, and technological integration, all relevant to my organization today. I personally found the content to be an excellent, practical complement on par to the theoretical knowledge I learned as an MBA graduate from the Wharton School at the University of Pennsylvania."

—Ming Khor, CEO of Keru

Maximizing Organizational Performance:
A Guide to Effective Performance Coaching
by Patrick Behar-Courtois, PhD

© Copyright 2025 Patrick Behar-Courtois, PhD

ISBN 979-8-88824-736-5

All rights reserved. No part of this publication may be reproduced, stored in a retrieval system, or transmitted in any form or by any means—electronic, mechanical, photocopy, recording, or any other—except for brief quotations in printed reviews, without the prior written permission of the author.

Published by

◤ köehlerbooks™

3705 Shore Drive
Virginia Beach, VA 23455
800-435-4811
www.koehlerbooks.com

MAXIMIZING ORGANIZATIONAL PERFORMANCE

A Guide to Effective Performance Coaching

PATRICK BEHAR-COURTOIS, PHD

VIRGINIA BEACH
CAPE CHARLES

TABLE OF CONTENTS

Introduction ... 1
Chapter I: Understanding Performance Coaching ... 7
Chapter II: Identifying Performance Gaps and Developing Coaching Plans ... 25
Chapter III: Providing Feedback and Supporting Development ... 36
Chapter IV: Leadership Coaching ... 44
Chapter V: Team Dynamics and Collaboration ... 55
Chapter VI: Employee Engagement and Retention ... 65
Chapter VII: Supporting Organizational Change ... 76
Chapter VIII: Promoting Diversity and Inclusion ... 87
Chapter IX: Adapting Coaching Strategies for Remote and Hybrid Work Environments ... 96
Chapter X: Measuring Success and Continuously Improving Coaching Programs ... 106
Chapter XI: Implementing and Sustaining Coaching Programs ... 117
Chapter XII: Sustaining a Culture of Coaching ... 123
Chapter XIII: Integrating Technology Into Performance Coaching ... 129
Chapter XIV: Future Trends ... 135
Chapter XV: Supporting Performance Coaching with the Right Tool Kit ... 142
Conclusion ... 207

INTRODUCTION

I'll never forget the knot I used to get in my stomach every Sunday night before the workweek started. It was literally survival of the fittest in telecom retail back when I first started working in my early twenties. We were all sharks, relentlessly circling and snapping at any opportunity to get an edge on our competitors.

Looking back, I realize my behavior was unproductive and detrimental to the team. Always putting intense pressure on them to come up with the next big idea that would help us "blow the others out of the water." That was my rallying cry, as cringeworthy as it is to admit now. Looking back, that obsessive hunger to stay ahead of the curve was both my greatest strength and biggest weakness. On one hand, it turned me into a maniacally driven force that helped our company land massive deals and market share. But it also bred an extremely toxic, unsustainable work culture where burnout was inevitable.

It took hitting rock bottom and losing my job for me to come to my senses. I realized that sort of myopic, win-at-all-costs mentality was ultimately counterproductive in the long run. True success isn't just about having that shiny, trendy new product in the workplace. It also requires a more holistic and sustainable approach, working to optimize *all* aspects of the operating environment and workplace. Otherwise, we're just treading water until the next disrupter inevitably comes along. We live and learn, I guess.

From that lowest low, I gained a hard-earned perspective: Fostering an organizational culture hyperfocused on upskilling, innovation, and employee development is the key competitive advantage in today's volatile work environment. Dismissing this practice is akin to hoisting up a big neon sign blaring, *We're circling the drain over here!* It's all about nurturing an entire organizational ecosystem that can adapt and evolve to meet new problems and realities head-on.

Yes, being efficient and agile is the name of the game now. Companies that are successfully keeping ahead understand that the smartest way to run a business is to create a true learning organization—an organization in which everyone is focused on continuing to up their game and their operations. This culture focused on continual learning is critical to, sooner or later, keeping the competition at bay. We live in a VUCA[1] world, and complacency in such a context is the kiss of death. If you allow "business as usual" in the twenty-first century, you can be sure nothing out of the ordinary will happen to you, or your organization.

This is where performance coaching comes in. It provides the structured, guided mechanism employees need to seriously enhance their performance, hone their skills, and buy in to a culture of continuous improvement. Now, with principles rooted deeply in behavioral science and business smarts, quality performance coaching isn't going to come cheap. But it's high time organizations stopped viewing it as just another overhyped, expensive fad. It's a must-have for any company serious about achieving lasting success.

---

[1] VUCA stands for volatility, uncertainty, complexity, and ambiguity. The term originated in the US military in the 1990s and has since been widely adopted in business and organizational contexts to describe challenging and dynamic environments.

Performance coaching is a powerful tool for helping individuals and teams realize their full potential, and employees feel way more connected to their organization's mission as a result. They develop strategies to barrel through obstacles, and their performance levels go through the roof. It's all about using productive goal setting and feedback to maximize what your people are capable of. But it goes one huge step further by ensuring they have all the support and information needed to actually make those transformations happen.

I recall when I first experienced this as a manager years ago. We had this one rockstar employee, Amanda, who was an absolute beast at sales. However, she struggled with other key areas like client relationships and time management. Instead of just giving her vague feedback in our quarterlies, we worked together to pinpoint the specific skills she needed to improve. Then we built a customized coaching plan, though we did not call it that, to double down on those weaknesses while capitalizing on her closing strengths.

It was like night and day. Amanda went from feeling aimless and frustrated to laser focused. Her engagement levels skyrocketed as she could tangibly see areas of improvement. And, what do you know, within a couple of quarters her performance was through the roof—better client retention, more sales than ever before. She was just unstoppable.

Success stories like Amanda's demonstrate the immense value of performance coaching. When you take the time to highlight an employee's biggest growth opportunities and provide specialized, high-impact guidance, it doesn't just boost their engagement, it unlocks remarkable performance gains, increased productivity, and real, measurable business results. Boom.

But that's not all performance coaching brings to the table. While it benefits the employees by giving them a clear career pathway, it's a huge win for the company too. You get to retain your top talent and start building a leadership pipeline stocked with future leaders. It's a virtuous cycle.

Here's the thing—when individuals unlock their potential, the entire organization feels that positive ripple effect. That's why performance coaching aims to ensure employees' goals are tightly aligned with the company's strategic objectives, everyone working toward the same unified vision of success. Performance coaching creates a culture of continuous improvement that permeates every level of the organization. With regular performance evaluations, constructive feedback, and new goals being consistently set, your people will have no choice but to keep building their skills, driving maximum performance and delivering elite results.

This cycle of constant refinement is what allows companies to stay innovative, adaptable, and fiercely competitive in today's relentless business climate.

And, don't forget, employees who get that one-on-one performance coaching become way more engaged with their work, their organization, and the people coaching them. They feel valued and supported. Job satisfaction goes up, loyalty amplifies, and now you've got a workforce that actually wants to stick around. In a globalized economy where top talent is a company's biggest competitive advantage, making sure you retain your rising stars is absolutely crucial. The costs of continuously backfilling those roles are devastating.

Last but not least, performance coaching isn't just for the frontline workers. Leaders and managers deserve this kind of individualized development too. It helps them elevate their leadership abilities, sharpen those decision-making skills, and become unstoppable at driving team performance and crushing those big-picture, strategic goals.

Purpose and Objectives of the Book

This book aims to provide you with the tools and insights necessary to effectively leverage performance coaching in your organization. We're talking a clear road map for developing resources, techniques, and best practices to establish coaching programs that create meaningful, ongoing performance improvements for individuals, teams, and your entire organization.

My aim is to give you a no-BS breakdown of implementing performance coaching that actually works. We'll start by laying the foundations—what performance coaching is and why it matters so much for organizational and individual success.

From there, you'll get practical hands-on tools and techniques for identifying performance gaps, setting sustainable goals, and developing coaching plans that actively move the needle.

You're also going to develop a deep understanding of how to provide constructive feedback that resonates and growth strategies that truly empower your people's development. We'll look at how to effectively measure coaching impact, too, so you can keep optimizing and evolving your programs.

And, most importantly, I'll be giving you a bounty of real-world examples and case studies pulled from all kinds of industries and contexts. These cases don't just illustrate how performance coaching works in practice, they're inspiring nuggets you can adapt and mold to fit your organization's unique needs.

Target Audience and Intended Use

For HR professionals, this book serves as a comprehensive guide to enhancing team performance and morale through coaching. You'll learn to pinpoint weaknesses with sniper-like precision and discover effective coaching strategies to elevate everyone's game. Those daily coaching conversations will transform into high-impact growth opportunities.

Talent-development professionals will learn how to identify and fully utilize their high-potential employees, creating a strong pipeline of leaders that will help the organization continue to thrive into the future.

Now for all the consultants and coaches out there, this book shares insights that will reinvigorate how you deliver value. You'll discover, or rediscover, fresh angles and techniques to ensure your guidance actually sticks and creates lasting impact for your clients.

And to all the executives and managers: Consider these pages your playbook for weaving coaching into the very fabric of your leadership style. We'll make performance coaching feel as natural and instinctive as checking your email in the morning.

By the time you've finished, you will have a strategically tailored set of high-impact plays to drive your organization's success.

Whatever your perspective—whether you're just starting out, or you're an experienced professional—I hope the insights in these coming pages will spark new fire and fresh ideas to inspire you to take your next leap.

CHAPTER I

Understanding Performance Coaching

Opening Case: Transforming Customer Service and Retention

Consider a retail organization in the UK facing high employee turnover and inconsistent customer service, both of which have affected its bottom line. To address these issues, the company initiates a comprehensive performance-assessment program as the first step in their coaching initiative. Managers conduct 360-degree feedback, customer surveys, and direct observation to gather detailed performance data on each employee. The assessments reveal key areas needing improvement, including communication skills and product knowledge.

Based on these insights, coaches are brought in to develop individualized coaching plans for employees, including specific goals and action steps. Employees participate in weekly coaching sessions that focus on addressing their unique performance gaps. Coaches provide continuous feedback and monitor progress through regular check-ins and performance reviews.

As a result, customer-service ratings improve significantly. Employees show substantial improvements in customer-interaction skills and product knowledge. Turnover rates decrease as employee engagement and satisfaction increase, leading to a boost in overall performance and higher productivity.

Overview and Definition

I'll never forget my first coaching session. I was just a bright-eyed, clean-cut junior marketing coordinator at the French headquarters of a Fortune 500 company. I had just come out of business school and thought I'd soon be running the world. Well, shortly after I started the job, I found myself sitting across from my manager, Francis, nervous and sweating as I prepared to receive the beating I was sure would inevitably come.

You see, I had always been the type of person who thrived on external validation. While I was not the most dedicated student in high school, I made a point to obtain my MBA and PhD degrees from top 1 percent business schools. I excelled at sports. I practiced several martial arts, swam, and surfed, all at competitive level. I had been offered this full-time role after only a four-month-long internship with this company, which had never been seen before.

I can't say that I was very comfortable with constructive criticism or having my shortcomings brought to light. It was downright terrifying. However, as Francis pulled up my information on his computer screen, I caught a hint of a smile on his face. "OK, Patrick," he said, leaning forward. "Let's talk about your goals."

I blinked in surprise. Goals? What about the way I agonize over a project until I no longer want to do it at all? What about the way I shut down every time I have a conflict with someone in the office? What about the way I choke on words in big team meetings for fear of looking stupid? But as Francis pressed on, asking me about my future career plans, what my strengths were, and, yes, what my weaknesses were, I felt something shift inside me. He wasn't there to tear me down or poke holes in everything I was doing wrong. He was there to listen, to understand, and to help me chart a path forward.

Over the course of our coaching relationship, I tackled projects that pushed me far outside my comfort zone. I remember one particularly harrowing presentation to the French executive team where I had to pitch a completely new way to calculate the incentive payments for their entire sales force. We're talking about a multimillion-euros budget being handled by a twenty-three-year-old kid. I was sure I would bomb it, but Francis helped me prepare, role-playing tough questions and reminding me of my unique value proposition.

And you know what? I nailed it. Yes, I was proud of myself for nailing the presentation, but most importantly I was proud to realize that I was capable of a lot more than I had ever given myself credit for. This had a huge impact on me.

Still, my coaching journey with Francis wasn't all a walk in the park. I had moments of frustration, of feeling down on myself, of almost quitting my job. I recall one quarter where I missed a key deadline on a major product launch. I was a young man having landed a coveted role and fending for myself in a highly political company, on an almost-daily basis. It felt like being dumped in a shark tank and having to learn to swim on my own, day in and day out. The stress, the pressure—something had to give, and, for me, it materialized in forgetting this critical deadline. I was sure Francis would be furious. But instead, he sat me down and helped me dissect what had gone wrong. I shared the pressure I was feeling, the way my coworkers seemed to set me up for failure, the impact I felt it could have on my future relationships with the sales force and other members in the organization. And together we brainstormed strategies to avoid similar missteps in the future.

Looking back now, I see those coaching sessions with Francis as a turning point in my career and my life, encouraging me to own my natural strengths, confront my fears, and believe in myself. There have been many managers and mentors since, but Francis will always be the first for whom I recall the transformational impact of the coaching experience.

Fast forward a few years and a few positions, and I was the person sitting on the other side of the table, now a manager tasked with coaching my own team members comprising individuals much, much older than me. Yes, I was terrified at first. What if I said something wrong? What if I wasn't able to help them like my coach helped me? That's when I started leaning into the principles and practices I had learned, and I watched—like magic—as people on my team grew. They took responsibility for their own development. They brought innovative ideas to the table. And they supported me and each other in ways that took the entire team to new levels of performance.

Did I face obstacles along the way? Of course. Coaching isn't a magic wand that solves every problem overnight. It takes time, consistency, and sometimes tough feedback on the part of the leader. One time I became aware that someone in my group was missing deadlines, and the work coming in wasn't at the same level as it had been before. I could have come down on the employee right away. However, instead, I started with curiosity. What was going on with this person? What could I do to help them get back on track? Through coaching conversations, I learned that the employee was having some personal challenges at home—and that these concerns not only affected their ability to focus at work, but ultimately their quality of output. Over time, through those conversations, we developed a list of strategies that they could use to better manage their time and stress levels; I also connected them with resources for additional support.

It didn't immediately solve the problem, but, six months

later, I watched this employee's performance and engagement soar. They felt seen, supported, and empowered to take control back. And that, to me, is the true power of coaching.

So, allow me to let you in on a little secret that's going to revolutionize the way you support your employees. It's called performance coaching, and I can assure you, it's a total game changer.

I can see you wondering: *Another buzzword from one of these MBA guys? Just another fad, another flavor-of-the-month initiative? No way!*

But don't worry, performance coaching is different. It's a critical tool, one that can change the way your people show up and perform every day. Keep in mind—you're a coach, a manager, or an HR practitioner. Someone tasked with facilitating personal bests. Someone who is expected to help employees reach their wildest career aspirations. That's what performance coaching is really all about.

Performance coaching is a dynamic, collaborative process that assists employees in achieving their goals and results by understanding where they are now and where they want to be, then giving them the tools to get there. Now, performance coaching is not a one-and-done proposition; rather it's a personal, collaborative relationship between you and the employee. As a coach, you are the employee's mentor, sounding board, and supporter. Your role is to support and encourage, and to hold them accountable throughout the process.

But that doesn't mean that performance coaching is about hand-holding your employees. On the contrary, it's about empowering them to take charge of their own growth, giving them the support and key resources they need to hit the ground running, and then knowing when to step back to let them do it.

And even better, performance coaching isn't just for senior executives or high potentials. It's a tool you can use for your entire workforce. It concerns everybody in an organization, from the top to bottom! Whether you're working with a new employee just beginning their journey, or an experienced manager ready to take their leadership abilities to the next level, performance coaching will help you start where your employees are and get them to where it is they want to go. And yes, you are probably already very busy and have a million things to do. So, it might be natural to think that performance coaching is one more burden you need to carry. But performance coaching isn't a task, it's an investment. An investment in your people, in your organization, and in your own leadership skills. And when you make that investment, the payoff is huge.

You'll see your employees showing up to work with refreshed intensity and enthusiasm, stretching themselves in new directions and taking on the kinds of challenges that enable the most growth. Most importantly, you'll see them achieving results that they never thought possible. And this is exactly what you do as a coach or HR professional—help your people be their best self, driving the organization forward along the way.

So, if you're not yet using performance coaching as a part of your leadership tool kit, you know what to do: start now. And if you are, keep it up! Keep pushing yourself to be the best coach you can be, and keep empowering your employees to shoot for the moon. Because, after all, that's what any good leader is really supposed to be doing: motivating, energizing, and elevating others. And with performance coaching in your tool kit, there's no limit to how far you and your team can go.

The Coaching Process

Let's have a look at what this coaching process looks like. It's not just a random set of steps thrown together; all parts have to be clearly defined and followed in order for employees to fully grow and develop.

But before we jump in, we need to get a solid grasp on where the employee is at right now. It reminds me of this one time when I was invited by a large service company to coach a team leader named Lin. She was really struggling. Her numbers were way down, and her team was just . . . well, they were kind of losing steam. Morale was basically in the dumps. So, one day—this was after a particularly rough team meeting, I believe—I pulled her aside and asked: "Lin, listen. I want to sit down. You and me. Coffee? I want to hear your thoughts on how things are going, what you feel like you're crushing, and where you might need a little extra support right now."

And it was great. Just by putting that on the table and really delving into her performance, we started seeing all these places where she needed help. Together, we looked at her performance reviews, got 360-degree feedback from her team and colleagues on areas viewed as priorities for development, and then took the time to have her do a self-assessment. It was like detective work—we had all these clues and put them together to see the full picture.

And that's the thing about performance coaching, right? We've got this whole arsenal of tools and techniques to help us understand an employee's current performance, yet the key is to stay objective. We're not allowed to let our own biases color the picture. Be objective. Keep it real, keep it straight—keep it honest, as we say—and see where they are, so we know where to take them. And sometimes, that takes some hard truths and hard questions. Still, that's what we're here for as performance coaches: to help our employees grow, even when it's uncomfortable.

With that assessment in hand, now comes the next part—setting goals! That is, the coach and employee identifying and agreeing on SMART goals. These goals don't just materialize out of thin air. They need to be grounded in reality. Yes, they have to do with the employee, but more importantly they have to do with the job, the day-to-day, and also the company and its mission, vision, and future. That's why these SMART targets are so critical: They basically provide the employee with a clear picture of what they're working toward, what success looks like, and how they can do it. It's all about setting them up to win and giving them the tools and the knowledge they need to excel.

Next, we've got the action plan. This is like the employee's personal road map to success. It sets out the steps the employee will need to take, the resources they'll need to deploy, and the timeline for getting it all done. Yet, the coach stands right alongside the employee, offering informative feedback and direction, and cheering them along every step of the way. Importantly, the feedback offered needs to be effective and on point. We're talking specific, timely, and focused on behaviors and actions. None of this "lacking optimism" nonsense that doesn't actually tell us anything useful. I mean real, specific, action-focused feedback.

Finally, we measure the employee's improvement, bringing back key metrics; gather feedback on the employee's experience (as well as their peers'); and eventually call out coaching points and whether they've been effective. Measuring coaching success, which we'll explore in-depth later, is crucial for program effectiveness. This really comes down to the idea that coaching either needs to be effective or terminated, and areas of improvement can manifest from reviewing coaching involvement.

Now, I know what you're thinking. *One size fits all, right?* Wrong! Performance coaching comes in all shapes and sizes. You've got your classic one-on-one sessions, group coaching, peer coaching, virtual coaching—you name it. The approach you take depends on what the organization needs, what the employee's goals are, and the coach's personal style.

Key Principles

So, what makes performance coaching really work? It isn't as simple as setting a few targets and giving someone feedback, right? No, of course not. There's a bit of alchemy to the art and craft of it all. And there are some key principles and best practices that you should know if you want to master it.

First and foremost, when you set goals, they need to be very clear and readily measurable. There's no room for ambiguity. Fuzzy goals are for fuzzy minds, not people who are trying to make a difference. Now, bonus points if those goals are directly tied to the employee role and the organization's goals. If employees know exactly where they are supposed to be heading, it's like a shining beacon.

But here's the thing—coaching is a partnership, a collaboration. The coach brings the knowledge, the guidance, the tools, the support. And what about the employee? Well, the employee's got to bring the ownership and energy and vision to do the work. And, frankly, a performance coach can't do much for someone who doesn't want to be coached. That's just the reality of things, and no honest coach will disagree with that.

I'm also a huge believer in playing to people's strengths. If you focus on someone's strengths, they start shining in their role, they enjoy it, and they work harder. Still, that doesn't mean you hide the growth areas. It's all about balance. You celebrate the strengths and work on the growth opportunities together.

And can we talk about feedback for a second? This is the area coaches mess up the most. We can't make feedback such a rare, mysterious thing. It's got to be regular, specific, actionable. And oh, please, please, *please*, make sure it's focused on behaviors and actions, not personal attributes. No one wants to hear that they're "just not enough," yada yada. Here's a secret few seem to know: People can work on their behaviors; however, they can't change their attributes. Tell them specifically what they can do differently, not that they should *be* different. It makes no sense.

Finally, performance coaching is a journey, a process that keeps evolving. Whatever you do, you've got to keep monitoring, getting feedback, and adjusting. The business environment is always changing, and performance coaching has to change with it. It's about transcending what used to work to continue to be effective, continuously.

Best Practices

If you want to be an effective performance coach, there are some established best practices that you mustn't ignore. A fancy title or a freshly obtained coaching certification won't get you very far without something more, something that connects you with your employees; trust and rapport are essential here.

For starters, you've got to create a safe space. For instance, imagine that you are having a coaching session with one of your employees. Call her Sarah. She is one of your high potentials, has been with the company for a few years now, yet you can tell lately that she's been somehow . . . off. Disengaged, maybe even a little unhappy.

First, as a coach, your job is to foster a space in which Sarah is comfortable opening up to you. Not in the "here's a sofa, lie down" sense, but in the all-important "I feel completely safe telling you my troubles" sense. You want her to know that she can share with you the good, the bad, and the ugly, whether it's a gnarly project at work or an absolutely wild ambition that she doesn't want to share with anyone else. Your job is to make that possible.

And here's the key: You have to do it without judgment. That means no eye-rolling, no constructive criticism or mean-spirited comment; it's just you listening, comprehending, and caring. Nothing else.

I learned this the hard way, by screwing up with an early coaching client. His name was Mark, and he was brilliant, albeit a bit prickly. In our first couple of sessions, he concluded—correctly—that I was frustrated with him, and that I wasn't meeting him where he was at. I'd cut him off, or I'd give him advice he hadn't asked for. Unsurprisingly, Mark shut down pretty quickly. It wasn't until I learned to put my own ego aside and solely listen that things started to shift. I remember one session where Mark came in looking really agitated. Instead of jumping in with solutions, I just sat back and said, "Hey, you seem like you've got a lot on your mind. Want to talk about it?"

And how he did! It came pouring: the stress he was under, the pressure he felt to perform, the fear of not being good enough. When Mark emerged from this session ninety minutes later, he was a different man—lighter, more open, ready to tackle his challenges head-on.

That's the power of creating a safe space. When your employees know they can come to you without fear of judgment or repercussion, that's when the real work can begin.

Still, you also have to bear in mind that performance coaching needs to be person-based. Every employee needs and uses different approaches, in that they are unique, with their own strengths, weaknesses, and even learning styles, which we'll discuss later. It's your job to first figure out which approach works best for each person. Get to know them. But most of all, get to know where they're coming from and where they want to go. And if you discover that you and an employee are out of sync? Send them to another coach. It's not about your ego, it's about what will work best for that employee. Now, I know some coaches who hold on for dear life, clinging to the relationship even if it isn't working. They let pride and greed take hold and go against what is good for the employee. That is a sure way to tank your coaching credibility. You've got to be willing to put your employees' needs first, always.

Another hallmark of good coaching? Encourage self-reflection and ownership. You cannot make an employee grow, no matter how much they might need it; they have to grow as a result of their own desires. All you can do is ask the right questions, prompt them to look inward, and help them identify their own areas of improvement. When they take ownership of their development, that's when the real magic happens.

And what about confidentiality? When an employee is in a coaching session with you, they're entrusting what's going on in there. They're conveying their vulnerabilities, mistakes, and fears—and they're expecting that what they say in the room will stay in the room. If they think that you'll be running straight to their boss at the end of every coaching session, it's over. They don't trust you. The relationship is dead.

All of which leads to the question: How on earth do you put all of this together? Well, with some structure and, perhaps today, some technology. Follow a clear process—assess, set goals, make a plan, give feedback, and evaluate. Leverage virtual coaching platforms and performance-tracking software to help you stay organized and efficient. And nowadays, there are more than enough commercial or open-source solutions to help you. However, don't let technology replace you, either. At the end of the day, performance coaching is still about holding a mirror up to someone and asking them to take a good hard look at themselves.

The Benefits for Organizations and Individuals

If you're not already implementing performance coaching in

your organization, it's time to do so. Because it works. Not only for organizations and institutions. But for people too.

First, there's a performance benefit. If you invest in performance coaching, it means that we are giving your people the gift of increased skill and the ability to hit their targets. We're supporting them with a market-tested, scientific approach to personal excellence. Truly, performance coaching puts your people ahead of those who don't receive coaching; I have seen it time after time.

And yet it's not all about the numbers. Coaching is also a tremendous employee-engagement tool. If you are taking the time to show your people that you value their growth and want them to develop, suddenly they start to feel appreciated and excited about work. In return, your organization will feel supercharged. It may sound obvious, but engaged employees don't quit. People who are engaged aren't spending any energy posting resumes or navigating to job boards or thinking about working somewhere else for so-and-so. They're in it for the long haul. That means lower turnover, and you can wave goodbye to the headaches and costs associated with new hires.

And wait, there's more! Performance coaching isn't just about preparing current contributors. It's also about developing the next generation of leaders. As you develop their competency to make decisions, communicate, and solve problems, you're building the leadership bench from the inside. And who doesn't want an extensive bench of talent ready to step up and lead?

Then there's the elephant in the room—culture. You know, the invisible yet omnipotent force that influences everything from how a decision is made, to which physical spaces foster a feeling of community. But guess what? *Voilà!* Performance coaching can also improve your organizational culture, helping employees be more curious, open to new ideas, and eager to work collaboratively. Fostering that culture—making coaching a norm that sustains performance improvement—is crucial, and we'll explore it more later.

Now, perhaps more importantly, performance coaching conditions your people to think and behave in ways that give them the flexibility and responsive determination they need to survive the unsettling new world we live in. It won't stop changing. It can't stop changing. Our only hope is that the people taking the helm of our organizations have been given the tools and the mindset to deal effectively with whatever change comes their way. Through performance coaching, you make your entire organization more agile and responsive. So, if you're not already investing in it, what are you waiting for? The ROI[2] is real. I've made my case. Still, don't just take my word for it. Talk to any organization that's made performance coaching a priority, and they'll tell you the same thing—"It's a total game changer."

And, if you're not an employee who gets assigned a performance coach, be proactive and advocate for yourself. Have the courage to say, "I'd really like to work with a coach. Are there any great ones here?" The investment in your career and personal development will be well worth it.

Potential Limitations and Challenges for Performance Coaches

As useful as performance coaching can be for employee development and organizational effectiveness, it's also important to acknowledge some of the potential limitations and challenges that may arise. Let's discuss a few challenges at the organizational level first.

One of the biggest obstacles is securing widespread buy-in. For performance coaching to stick, it's imperative that it be

---

[2] Return on Investment.

seen as a priority by managers and leaders at all levels of the organization. This requires a conscious commitment to allocating enough time, resources, and money to supporting coaching programs, as well as to communicating the benefits to employees. Without strong organizational commitment, coaching efforts may be seen as a "nice-to-have" rather than a strategic imperative.

Another potential challenge is ensuring a good fit between performance coaches and employees. Like any relationship, this dynamic relies heavily on chemistry, trust, and communication style, and the wrong coach for an employee—based on experience or expertise, style or interpersonal fit—can hinder the progress and ultimately undermine their engagement. For both individuals and organizations, making a good complementary match can be quite challenging.

Effective performance coaching also involves a commitment of time and resources. Sessions, goal-setting conversations, and feedback meetings all take employees away from the duties of the job. In fast-paced or resource-constrained environments, making room for coaching time can be difficult without overburdening ongoing work commitments and deliverables. Organizations need to be pragmatic about the time commitment required and ensure that employees have the necessary support and bandwidth to engage fully in the coaching process.

Finally, measuring the ROI of performance coaching can be complex, as key outcomes—the development of engagement, skills, and leadership capacity—are often intangible or long-term in nature. Without clear metrics or KPIs[3] in place, it can be difficult to justify the investment in coaching or to demonstrate its impact on individual and organizational performance. To overcome this, it's necessary for organizations to define clear success criteria for their coaching programs and track progress over time using a mix of quantitative and qualitative measures.

---

[3] Key Performance Indicators.

But performance coaches don't just run into issues at the organizational level, they also face a variety of challenges with their employees directly.

One of these common challenges is addressing employee skill gaps. When an employee is struggling significantly in their role, it's essential to quickly identify the skills or knowledge that they've completely and utterly lacked in their prior work history—because, unfortunately, you can't really tell what someone knows until they're hired. Your role is to identify those gaps and develop a targeted plan to help the employee acquire the necessary skills and knowledge. As with so many aspects of the job, it can be a challenge; however, the reward is great when that employee flourishes.

And then there is the motivational and engagement component. You'll spend time with employees who may be stuck, uninspired, and even a little hopeless. Your job will be to reignite their passion, formulate attainable targets, and cheer them on every step of the way. You will need to act as their personal hype squad, and trust me, you'll absolutely love it.

But the reality is that performance coaching isn't all unicorns and ice cream—communication can be challenging. There will be employees who are unable to clearly articulate a point, who avoid confrontation at all costs, and some, even, who have no idea how to listen. You don't get to demand that your employees get better at communication, and you can't force them to listen to your feedback until they explode. It's your job as a coach to teach them these communication skills and help them get through even the toughest conversations—active listening, giving and receiving constructive feedback, navigating conflict. It isn't always comfortable, but it's always worth it.

Then there's organizational change. You will be a critical resource to an employee who is trying to deal with this new role or team or process. You are there to help employees understand the reasons behind the change, develop coping strategies, and stay focused on their goals. As a facilitator of professional growth, you are essentially their GPS.

Another area where you'll be faced with an almost-universal challenge is plateaus in performance. Your employee will sometimes hit a "wall" and have no idea what to do about it. When employees reach a plateau, you'll help them break through barriers, set ambitious goals, and adopt a growth mindset. By providing guidance and support, you can help employees push past their limitations and reach new levels of performance.

Still, perhaps the most crucial coaching role you will come to play is as a facilitator of balance. Work, life, family, friends, pursuits—what's a person to do when it's all happening at once? Your employees will come to you for help in establishing strategies for time management, as well as for boundary setting and self-care. We're not talking about the heroic task of working harder here, but of working smarter.

And what about conflict within teams? When guiding your employees, your job will shift from mediator to referee to mediator again as you help team members talk through their problems, build sympathy for each other, and create solutions that work for everyone. It's not always going to be easy; however, high performance always requires it.

Finally, you'll sometimes work with people suffering from impostor syndrome. You know, people who don't feel like they measure up and won't until they do; they've been faking it 'til they make it and are looking to you for some encouragement. You'll tell these people they sound great. You'll compliment them on their accomplishments. You'll reframe their negative thoughts and help them develop a more positive self-image. To some extent, it's like being their personal cheerleader, always in their corner.

As we've explored the fundamentals of performance coaching, it's clear that identifying areas for improvement is crucial. In the next chapter, we'll delve into specific strategies for recognizing performance gaps and developing targeted coaching plans to address these areas.

CHAPTER II

Identifying Performance Gaps and Developing Coaching Plans

Opening Case: Boosting Sales Performance Across Stores

Consider an Australian retail chain struggling with inconsistent sales performance across its stores, which is affecting overall profitability. To address these issues, the company implements a coaching program focused on sales improvement. The company begins by reviewing sales-performance metrics across all stores to identify trends and outliers. Managers conduct targeted assessments, including direct observations, employee interviews, and mystery-shopper reports.

Based on their review of the assessments, coaches devise custom coaching plans for poorly performing stores by working with them on areas such as customer engagement and sales. The team of coaches puts together workshops for store managers and sales personnel on effective sales strategies and customer-service excellence. They also check in with the stores on a timely basis to give feedback, report progress, and amend the coaching program if necessary.

The stores that participate in the coaching program show significant improvements in sales performance, meeting or exceeding their sales targets. The customers at the stores experience better service and more knowledgeable staff, which heightens their satisfaction. The employees themselves also feel more confident and learn valuable skills. Therefore, the work environment becomes more pleasant as a result of the sales coaching program.

The Importance of Performance Assessment

Performance assessments are a critical component of any coaching plan, as they provide a clear picture of an employee's current strengths, weaknesses, and areas for improvement. Without this essential step, coaches may lack the insights needed to guide their employees effectively. After all, how can you expect to facilitate their travel if you don't even know where they're starting, and where they're actually trying to get? Yet that is what many of us attempt. Too often, we launch projects or teams into action without a proper map, relying on outdated reports or gut instinct to navigate the corporate terrain, hoping to course correct as obstacles emerge. And guess what? It hasn't delivered the results we need.

But when you do a thorough performance assessment? When you know your employee inside and out? That's when the magic happens. If you know exactly what your employee's strengths are, their areas of expertise, and the things they absolutely crush at work, you'll also know where they struggle, where they lack, and how they can be helped. And that's where you, coach, come in: Use that data to play to their strengths and shore up their weaknesses, tailoring your coaching plan to your highly individualized employee.

Of course, not all weaknesses are created equal. Some, like a deficiency in communication skills, can be improved with training and practice. But others, like a lack of competitiveness in a salesperson—that's a much tougher nut to crack. That's where your long years of consulting or managerial experience come in handy. That experience will help you know when to push and when to pivot.

Goal setting can be challenging, particularly when goals are not grounded in a realistic assessment of an employee's current performance and potential. You're setting someone up to fail before they even start. But once you do the assessment, that's when you can create those truly achievable goals, those that will stretch your employee without unduly stressing them out.

And don't forget feedback. A good performance assessment gives you the hard facts you'll need to provide specific, useful feedback that your employee can act on. You can point out what they're doing wrong, too—you can even create a road map to improvement.

And perhaps the best thing about performance assessments? You discover the potential superstars on your team, those ready to take on bigger assignments, become leaders, make a difference, if their individual goals align with where the organization is heading. That's when you know that all cylinders are firing.

⚴

Limitations and Pitfalls of Performance Assessments

While performance assessments can definitely help identify natural abilities, weaknesses and improvement areas, they are not immune to pitfalls.

One big risk is bias. It's sneaky and can creep in from all angles. I once worked with a manager who consistently gave high evaluations to team members he played golf with. Coincidence? I think not. Our personal relationships, preconceived ideas, or unconscious biases about race, gender, or age can really skew our judgment.

How, then, shall we counteract this? Standardized assessment tools can help; although, again, they're far from perfect. Another trick is to get input from multiple sources—peers as well as subordinates, customers and so on. The wider the array of sources, the fuller the picture becomes. One further suggestion: Have whatever assessments you're working with reviewed by someone independent from the coaching relationship. Fresh eyes can spot biases we might miss.

Another trap I've seen many fall into is using assessments as a stick rather than a carrot. An employee's motivation withers instantly if they think they are being punished for their weaknesses. I always tell my clients to frame assessments as a growth tool. It's not about pointing fingers; it's about identifying opportunities.

Lastly, don't lose sight of the fact that assessments are just a snapshot. They're useful, but they're not the whole story. I always encourage ongoing feedback, observation, and open dialogue. It's amazing what you can learn about an employee's potential over a casual coffee chat that you might miss in a formal assessment.

Techniques for Identifying Performance Gaps and Areas for Improvement

To effectively identify performance gaps and areas for improvement, it's important to use a diverse range of assessment techniques and tools. Keep in mind that this isn't a one-and-done kind of deal. It requires a systematic approach and a whole assessment tool kit to ascertain where your employees are exceeding expectations and where they may need development.

First, the good old annual review. You know, the one where the manager sits down with the employee to examine KPIs and goals and talk about how the individual contributed to the team. At its best (and by best, I mean more than just once a year), this annual review can provide some valuable insights about an individual's strengths and areas for development—again, if done properly with a manager who understands the value of such an approach, and, at the very least, twice a year.

But why end there? An authentic 360-degree assessment of one's performance involves data inputs from all sides—colleagues, superiors, subordinates, and, yes, other stakeholders. Each side offers a different view, and when you put all the pieces together, you have the whole picture.

And then, there is the power of self-reflection. Ask your employees to take a good hard look in the mirror and, if you phrase the questions correctly, you're bound to get some revealing ideas. Give them some questions to stew over, take them through simple yet powerful frameworks such as the Johari window (which we'll discuss further), or encourage them to do a personality test, and with any luck they'll start noticing things they didn't see before. Aha moment!

And what about those jobs that can't be done without the involvement of a customer or client? Here's where getting feedback from that external stakeholder (the customer or client) is really key, since they are perhaps the best person to provide feedback on how an employee is responding to customers in key areas such as service skills, communication style, problem-solving, and so on.

And for the record, let's talk numbers. Objective performance metrics such as dollar sales, production per hour, error rates, and completion of projects on time? They don't lie. Analyzing these performance metrics can highlight gaps that should receive immediate attention.

However, metrics are only part of the story, and that's where those behavioral observations come in. You can't simply set a goal and walk away. It's vital for a manager or performance coach to go out into the field and see how employees are executing on their task, how they're interacting with other people, how they're coping with a challenge while it's happening in front of us. Be a fly on the wall, but observe with purpose.

Finally, practitioner tools that measure competencies are not to be ignored. These instruments evaluate an employee's skills and abilities against predefined frameworks, allowing you to identify weaknesses that might prove crucial in the role they're doing, or the role they're being groomed for. Competency assessments also have the added advantage of possessing better predictive validity and reliability than personality-based solutions, which we'll explore later. In simple terms, they provide a clear, direct, and practical picture of how well a person is likely to perform a specific role based on a set of demonstrated skills and, ultimately, behaviors. And while traditional assessment methods are highly valuable, technology-based tools can provide even more comprehensive and real-time performance data.

Best Practices for Setting Performance Goals and Objectives

Let's now talk about one of the most powerful tools in our coaching arsenal: setting performance goals. Many of us feel the duty to do whatever we can to inspire our employees to greater heights.

So just what is a good goal, exactly? Well, a good goal is S-M-A-R-T. But I'm not talking about IQ points. Five simple words: specific, measurable, attainable, relevant, and time based. These are the building blocks for goals you'll actually stick to.

Imagine a scenario—one, I suspect, that will resonate for more than a few of you. You're a freshly graduated cook who's taken a job in a hot new restaurant that everyone's gushing about. Cool. Anyway, you're all dressed up in a sharp white chef's jacket and ready to wow the world with your culinary genius. But hold up! No one's told you what you're supposed to be cooking!

I mean, can you imagine? The gleaming cookware, the fridge bulging with fresh ingredients, you standing there like a deer in headlights, all: "Um, guys? A little assistance, please?" Sound familiar?

I've seen this scenario play out more times than I can count in my coaching career. I recall working with a top-notch operations whiz who was brought in to "shake things up" at his new company. Great! Except . . . nobody bothered to tell him what needed shaking. Talk about a recipe for disaster!

How many times in your career have you experienced this scenario yourself? Think carefully now. That feeling as if you're stuck and have no idea where to start, expected to conjure up brilliance with a mere flick of your wrist. Feeling frustrated as hell, I'm sure. It's not fair. Not even a little bit.

So, here's my challenge to all you leaders out there. Ask yourself the question: Are you giving your team the recipe for success? Or are you just throwing them into the kitchen and hoping for the best? Without guidance, we could be slicing with the wrong side of the blade or the wrong side of the bread. Direction is a need-to-have, not a nice-to-have. Without it we're all just poking around in the dark, hoping we'll land on something that works. Which of course isn't the way to run a business (or make a soufflé). So, setting SMART goals is a bit like turning on a powerful flashlight for our employees and pointing them to the right direction.

And another bit of magic: If we get our employees involved

in creating these goals, it's like giving them a sense of ownership over their own development. They aren't just standing there having a goal thrown at them. Now they're saying, "Wait a minute, let's actually create the performance-development plan." I've found, as a good coach would, that when people feel like they have some ownership in the development plan, they work harder.

Let's talk about clarity for a second. Any goal setting you do should make crystal balls green with envy. Your employees have to know just what you want them to do, and how you're going to measure them. No guessing, no ambiguity. Clear, measurable targets.

Also, we don't want to set the bar too low, or too high. It's a balancing act. We want to stretch our employees and push them out of their comfort zone, but we don't want to push them so far out that they feel like they're failing all the time. As performance coaches, it's essential to find that sweet spot.

But even more important than setting goals for here and now is recognizing that, as facilitators of professional growth, our job doesn't end there. Ensuring that goals don't devolve into mere number crunching and box ticking is essential; the strength of the goal-setting conversation is that it offers an opportunity to grow and develop employees not just this quarter, but for years to come. So, we coaches need to offer our employees constant, bidirectional feedback on their goals. We must walk beside them at all times, course correcting their goal-setting endeavors whenever they drift.

Finally, my beloved documentation. Yes, I know, it's as exciting as an exploratory dental procedure. Still, when you take the time to log your employee's goals and track them, you'll have a hidden motivation and accountability weapon in your back pocket.

Developing Effective Coaching Plans

But a goal without a plan is, what? A wish, I think. And that's where you come in with action steps. You have to break the plan down into measurables, like ingredients and steps in a recipe.

And timelines, you may ask? If there are no deadlines or milestones, it's pretty much the same as running a race with no finish line—you're going to keep running and running forever until you drop dead. So create those milestones; it's like lighting a fire under your employee's you-know-what. But the paradox is this: While your employee can begin this adventure alone, they cannot go on as a development lone ranger. They need resources. They need support. They need a cheering squad. And that's where you come in. You need to be their guide, their mentor, their biggest fan.

And then there's the feedback, which often dooms coaching plans. It's not set it and forget it—this step also requires you to check in, coach, and course correct along the way.

And how do you know if the employee is getting better at the objective? This is where the metrics come in—there needs to be a clear set of objective measures for success. If you're playing a game, and you don't know what the rules are—or how to keep score—how can you know if you're winning?

I know right now you might be thinking: *But what if things change? What if the plan doesn't work?* That's just the way life is. Being flexible and adaptable is an integral part of being a performance coach. If you need to pivot, pivot. If your recipe is no good, then change the recipe. The key is to stay agile and keep your eye on the prize.

And speaking of prizes, don't forget to throw some in along the way! Praising your employee's wins is like giving them a big fat gold star; it's motivation, it's reinforcement, it's a reminder to carry on the good work.

Using Assessment Data to Create Individualized Coaching Plans

Performance assessments provide coaches with rich data to support the creation of customized coaching programs. They gear up with the personalized knowledge of their employees' most tangible strengths, weaknesses, and areas of development to craft approaches that best fit their employees' specific needs and goals.

For example, take a marketing manager, David, who just received his 360-degree assessment results: David is appreciated for his skills in coming up with creative campaign ideas and developing good relationships with clients. However, he needs to develop better time-management and delegation skills. Raters also report that David has spread himself too thin and is not letting others take the lead. As a result, deadlines are being missed, and the environment is very stressful.

The coach uses this performance data to develop a tailored plan for David to improve his time-management skills and delegation capacities. This plan might involve the following:

- Giving him time-management tools or techniques (e.g., prioritization matrices or time-blocking strategies).

- Role-playing scenarios where he practices delegating tasks and providing clear instructions and expectations to his team members.

- Setting SMART goals that matter. For example: "Delegate at least three significant tasks a week to team members" or "Finish all projects at least two days prior to deadline."

- Pairing him with a mentor who is an expert at time management and delegation, and who can provide ongoing guidance and support.

The coach would then track David's progress (including setbacks), check in regularly with him, celebrate successes, and provide course corrections as he goes.

This shows how assessment data can be used to inform individualized coaching plans that will help an employee advance through clarifying the implications of their unique strengths, challenges, and goals. By taking the time to understand each employee holistically, and to create strategies and informal learning paths that build on these unique strengths, challenges, and goals, coaches can help them reach their full potential.

With a solid understanding of how to identify performance gaps and create coaching plans, we're now ready to tackle one of the most critical aspects of coaching: providing effective feedback. The next chapter will guide you through the art of delivering constructive feedback and supporting ongoing development.

CHAPTER III

Providing Feedback and Supporting Development

Opening Case: Supporting Development Through Feedback

Consider an advertising firm in Japan recognizing the need to enhance the leadership skills of its senior managers to improve decision-making and team performance. To address these issues, the firm implements a pilot leadership-coaching program. Coaches begin with 360-degree feedback to identify each manager's leadership strengths and areas for improvement. They then work with each manager to set specific goals, such as improving strategic decision-making and enhancing team communication.

Senior managers participate in biweekly coaching sessions, focusing on real-world scenarios and leadership challenges. The firm also organizes workshops on strategic thinking, effective communication, and conflict resolution. Continuous feedback is provided, helping managers reflect on their progress. As a result, managers report improved decision-making capabilities and greater confidence in handling complex situations. Teams led by coached managers show better performance and higher engagement levels. The program significantly boosts leadership competence within the firm, contributing to higher client satisfaction and increased efficiency.

The Role of Feedback in Performance Coaching

Have you ever had a boss or mentor who gave you really good feedback? I mean a real light bulb moment? I've been coaching for years, and the times I've really nailed giving feedback have been so gratifying.

Think about it: We are the coaches, and our people rarely get more candid feedback than from us. We have the opportunity to help them grow, get out of their comfort zones, and be better than they ever imagined they could be, and we do it through feedback.

But wait, I've already pegged your closing argument. You're probably thinking: *But isn't "feedback" just about telling people what they're doing wrong?* Au contraire, my friend! When done right, feedback is far more than that—it's about setting clear expectations, highlighting strengths, and providing a road map for growth.

Consider this scene. You're coaching an employee who hasn't been able to achieve a given goal. They don't know where to go or what to do next. Your feedback skills can literally help put them back on the map. As you provide an actionable picture of what they can do to succeed—how, specifically, things could have gone better—you're also equipping them with the GPS data to get them where they want to go.

Now, the other real magic of feedback is that your goal isn't just to tell people what they're doing wrong. It's also about recognizing and celebrating what your employees are doing right! When you highlight their strengths and achievements, you're giving them a massive confidence boost and reinforcing those rock star behaviors. Those same behaviors they're exhibiting or the same activities in which they're engaged are the ones you want to see, and with that feedback, you're calling attention to them, and you're saying, "Hey! Keep being awesome!"

And let's not forget the power of constructive feedback. It's tempting to avoid the tougher kinds of conversations; however, they really are important. When having these conversations, focus on being very specific about the areas you think they could improve upon and provide suggestions about how to do so. These "change" conversations are not sources of negativity, but rather are ways you can empower others on your team.

Of course, feedback is most powerful when it's part of a comprehensive development approach. That's why it works hand in hand with solid individual-development plans (IDPs), discussed later in chapter XV, that clearly outline goals and expectations. It's why the best coaches ensure their people have access to resources—workshops, courses, industry reading—to level up their skills. And it's why they create stretch assignments that might initially feel uncomfortable but ultimately reveal what employees are truly capable of.

Add in mentoring relationships and peer-support networks where your people can find guidance and encouragement, and you've created an environment where feedback doesn't just land—it transforms. When feedback is delivered in a culture that values growth mindset—the belief that skills develop through dedication and hard work—you've got a winning formula for helping your team reach their full potential.

Making Feedback a Two-Way Dialogue

Good feedback is a two-way conversation—not a lecture in which the coach has all the smarts and the employee listens.

Soliciting employee input and participation helps a

performance coach understand the person's issues, challenges, and needs more thoroughly so they can better inform the full range and depth of feedback and support that will be provided. Inviting employee participation also builds personal connection and shared accountability, as an employee is more likely to invest in change when they feel heard and valued.

It can help identify potential blind spots or areas where the coach's perception may differ from the employee's experience. This leads to more accurate and relevant feedback. And it also creates a safe, supportive environment where employees feel comfortable sharing their thoughts, asking questions, and taking risks.

To encourage employee participation, as coaches, we can ask questions like:

- "How do you feel about your performance on this project? What do you think went well, and what do you think could be improved?"

- "What challenges or obstacles did you face, and how did you try to overcome them?"

- "What support or resources do you need to be more successful in the future?"

- "How can I, as your coach, better support your growth and development?"

- "What are your thoughts on the feedback I've provided? Do you have any questions or concerns?"

- "What goals would you like to set for yourself based on this feedback, and how can I help you achieve them?"

When we ask open-ended questions and actively listen to our employees' responses, we create a dialogue that leads to more meaningful, actionable feedback and a stronger coaching relationship built on trust and collaboration. Also, while face-to-face feedback is ideal, in the globalized environment we now work in, these techniques can be adapted for remote teams using virtual platforms, as we'll explore in chapter IX.

Best Practices for Providing Constructive Feedback

Let's talk about the art of delivering constructive feedback that actually makes a difference.

First things first: Make the feedback specific and clear. Many people have received vague, unhelpful feedback from a manager in the past. Instead of helpful direction such as "That report was really weak. Last-quarter sales data is missing and the overall flow of the document is hard to follow," I once remember getting the wishy-washy "Ooh, Patrick, the report didn't quite do it for me." This feedback didn't give me, the recipient, any idea of what to fix. Better to say specifically: "You didn't include this, you didn't have that, or this part was wrong." Give the road map. Make it easy.

Another key thing to keep in mind: Focus on the behavior, not the individual. Saying "You're all over the place!" may be tempting, but it can be damaging to the person's self-esteem. Try instead: "I noticed you weren't able to keep the focus of our planned agenda back in that last meeting." See the difference? It's all about actions, not the self. It sounds less like an attack, more like facts.

Now, let's talk about timing. Providing feedback on an issue that occurred several months ago is unlikely to be effective or well received. Make a point to serve feedback piping hot and immediate to make it stick. The sooner you give feedback, the more relevant and impactful it will be.

But that doesn't mean the positive feedback loop should be forgotten about either. In fact, both the positive and negative reinforcement cycles have their places—especially when it comes to giving constructive (or positive or developmental) feedback. This approach to constructive feedback not only enhances individual performance, it also reinforces the coaching culture we'll explore later. And, if you happen to see an employee doing something great? Great—shout it from the rooftops (okay, a bit hyperbolic, but you catch my drift). Celebrating wins and strengths is every bit as important as it is to look at and minimize weaknesses and failures.

Overcoming Common Challenges in Providing Feedback and Support

Providing feedback and support can be difficult. I mean, we've all been there—you're trying to help an employee grow, but they're not exactly thrilled to hear what you have to say. Try giving a dog a bath. It's not always pretty, but it's necessary.

How, then, do we manage these choppy waters and ensure an employee feels respected on the other side of the table? The answer comes back to that positive vibe, that good feeling, that safe place where you're completely open with each other. Some people call it a feedback nest, and it really is that.

One way to do this is to really emphasize that your feedback is coming from a good place. You're not trying to criticize or attack them. You really do want them to be successful and good at their job—you're on their side, remember? The SBI model is a big help here, giving the vague kudos comments some real, concrete substance. Rather than just generalized praise, you're showing them the specifics of situations, behaviors, and impacts. You're basically holding up a mirror and saying, "Look, this is what I see, and here's how it's affecting things."

Of course, sometimes employees might not even realize they need to improve. They're looking only at their immediate surroundings, wearing blinders to their development path—think of how unaware racehorses are to the scenery of grandstands and crowds. That's where self-reflection comes in. Encourage them to take a good hard look at themselves and their work. There are many tools available to help, such as 360-degree feedback, personality assessments, and self-assessment questionnaires. Consider it a personal GPS system to help them navigate their own growth.

But what if they get defensive or upset? Yes, it happens, and be prepared for it. Feedback is tough to accept for some, and it can definitely be an emotional minefield. However, this is your chance to do it as sensitively and empathetically as possible. Tell them that it's OK to feel vulnerable or upset; let them feel, vent even; and make sure that you focus on the what, not on the who, the behavior, not the human being.

Another thing to keep in mind is the balance between positive and constructive feedback. You don't want to be the kind of coach who only dwells on the negative. That's just a recipe for a demoralized employee. At the same time, don't let them leave feeling like they were getting a nice syrupy massage at the spa. It's a delicate dance, but the "feedback sandwich" approach can be a lifesaver. Start with something positive, then slide in the constructive feedback, and end on a high note. It's like wrapping the tough stuff in a warm fluffy blanket of positivity. I say "fluff" because you don't want the constructive feedback totally buried—that's absolutely not the idea here. You just want it cushioned.

Of course, none of this works if you're not consistent and fair. If you're giving one employee tough love and another one gets a free pass, you'll welcome some serious problems, including trust issues. So, make sure you've got clear standards and criteria in place, and stick to them. Use hard data and evidence to back up your feedback, and treat everyone the same. You are a feedback referee: You see the foul, the pass, the shot on the net. And you've got to call it as you see it.

Finally, nurture a feedback-friendly culture. Some employees might be afraid to seek it out, because they see feedback as some kind of monster crouched under their beds, waiting to jump out and attack them. If you can show them that feedback isn't scary, that it's actually a beneficial, nurturing thing, a tool for growth and development, that can make all the difference. Do it yourself: Ask for feedback and show how you willingly use it to improve yourself.

Last but not least, let's not forget the power of celebration! When people come to you for feedback, make it a big deal. Celebrate it, reward it, show them that it's valued and appreciated. And when your employees hit those targets and deliver an extraordinary achievement, it's time to break out the confetti and let them know how proud you are. You'll find that a little recognition is worth a whole lot more than you realize as you keep that motivation engine humming.

Effective feedback is the cornerstone of performance coaching, yet it takes on special significance when applied to leadership roles. In the following chapter, we'll explore how to tailor coaching techniques for leaders at various levels of an organization.

CHAPTER IV

Leadership Coaching

Opening Case: Developing Strategic-Leadership Skills

Consider a UK financial services firm that wants to help its senior leaders become better strategists in order to improve decision-making and to stimulate business growth. To address these issues, the firm introduces a strategic-leadership coaching program. The firm initiates a program that begins with a needs assessment to identify gaps in the leaders' strategic-thinking abilities. Coaches then develop tailored coaching plans focusing on strategic planning, market analysis, and decision-making under uncertainty.

Leaders engage in a six-month, biweekly program of one-to-one performance coaching, which includes sessions on strategic scenario planning and real-time problem-solving; workshops on strategic frameworks and tools—for example, SWOT[4] (strengths, weaknesses, opportunities, threats), the BCG[5]

---

[4] The SWOT analysis framework, often attributed to research conducted at the Stanford Research Institute in the 1960s, helps organizations assess internal and external factors affecting their performance.

[5] The BCG Matrix, developed by the Boston Consulting Group, helps classify business units or products based on market growth and market share.

and Ansoff[6] Matrices, the Balanced Scorecard[7], and competitive strategy; and regular feedback on the progress of aligning team function to team and organizational strategic goals. As a result, leaders develop stronger strategic-thinking abilities and improve their decision-making skills. The firm experiences notable business growth due to better strategic decisions and a more proactive approach to market opportunities. In addition, the program helps develop a pipeline of future leaders equipped with strong strategic capabilities.

The Importance of Leadership Coaching

Let's talk about a powerful tool in our coaching arsenal: leadership coaching. As a coach, you know that helping leaders reach their full potential is a critical part of driving organizational success. Still, how exactly does leadership coaching work its magic?

If you're coaching a leader, you are in fact coaching a network. Not only are you helping that leader improve their individual capacities (yes, this very much needs to be part of the equation), but your work is affecting people beyond their direct reports, even beyond their area of responsibility, and certainly beyond the organization. What if a leader shapes strategy and work with greater clarity? What if they make better decisions? What if they inspire and motivate their teams? What if they manage these things better and smarter? You're essentially helping them create a ripple effect that touches every corner of the organization.

---

[6] The Ansoff Matrix, introduced by Igor Ansoff, is a strategic tool for identifying growth opportunities by analyzing product and market combinations.

[7] The Balanced Scorecard, introduced by Robert Kaplan and David Norton, provides a comprehensive framework for measuring organizational performance across financial, customer, internal process, and learning perspectives.

Equally important for the value of leadership coaching is the fact that it inspires more than just improving the present moment in leadership. This is where your role as a performance coach becomes significant, identifying and developing future talent—those individuals termed "high potentials" (or "HiPos," for short)—those people that demonstrate potential for receiving future assignment to positions that hold greater levels of organizational authority. Manage them well. The more distinctive your HiPos, the more valuable the process of grooming them, ensuring the broader organization remains viable and dynamic by putting individuals into the right positions at the right time.

Of course, being a leader can be tough. There will be challenges, roadblocks, and curveballs, and oftentimes leaders may feel like their mettle is being tested. This is where performance coaching comes into its own: the skills, strategies, and ways of thinking that enable leaders to change, deal with difficulties, and rise up even better leaders than before. This isn't only about how personal and professional challenges can be mastered; it's also about instilling a culture where creativity, innovation, and continuous improvement become the norm. When you coach leaders to create a positive, forward-thinking, and innovative atmosphere, you create fertile ground for breakthroughs, new approaches to problems, and entrepreneurial change.

And there is alignment. In your coaching role, you can clarify direction for leaders by communicating strategic imperatives, and help them, as employees, feel as though they're in the same boat rowing to a common destination. They feel more engaged, and performance increases.

Thus, leadership coaching is not about working one-on-one with an individual to develop them; it's about transforming organizations by transforming leaders. Get it right and you're developing the very best versions of your leaders, creating a positive spiral that makes a brighter future for everyone inside the organization.

And it's crucial to note that coaching is not just about sharing knowledge and advice—it's also critically important for helping leaders create a psychologically safe environment where they can explore, discover, and reflect on their own potential. Create a safe environment, ask thought-provoking questions, and allow leaders the space to explore, discover, and grow.

Ultimately, leadership coaching is about building a legacy of great leaders that can help an organization succeed for years to come.

Enhancing Leadership Skills and Decision-Making Through Performance Coaching

As facilitators of professional growth, we have the unique opportunity to help leaders unlock their full potential and make a powerful difference in their organizations. And it's pretty powerful stuff to be a part of.

The first area of work for leadership coaching is in building confidence—helping create conditions in which leaders discover their potential and feel confident making the tough decisions required to lead teams through tough situations. I'll never forget my coaching work with a senior manager in a manufacturing firm during a challenging corporate restructuring. His and his team's prospects looked highly uncertain, and he was all but a driver of change for his organization. However, during our coaching sessions, he gained a clear understanding of the need for change and, more importantly, the confidence to navigate that transition like a true leader. Watching him grow and succeed stands out as one of the highlights of my coaching career.

However, confidence is only part of the game. As coaches,

we also have the opportunity to help leaders develop strategic-thinking skills that will elevate their decision-making to new heights. I have seen this at a large market research firm. Coaching the senior managers on strategic planning and walking through various case studies on the job helped them see the bigger picture with their decision-making, in turn aligning more effectively with the goals of the organization.

Now, let's turn to communication and emotional intelligence—among the most crucial skills for any leader. In coaching a leader, consider how to incrementally hone their ability to get ideas and inspiration across with clarity and impact, while also bolstering the empathy, self-awareness (including of potential biases in their coaching approach, as discussed in chapter VIII), and social-emotional expertise needed to develop rapport and mutual trust with members of the team.

Creating a Psychologically Safe Environment Through Coaching

Performance coaching helps to create a psychologically safe environment where leaders can be candid about what is on their mind, where they feel comfortable taking risks, knowing they will be protected if the attempt fails, and where they can be vulnerable and make mistakes and still be OK. This is the kind of environment where trust and open communication—along with learning, growth, and innovation—can thrive.

We need to establish a deep level of trust, by first having a strong, solid, and supportive relationship with the leader's employees. Such a relationship creates a safe zone for leaders to let go, to unload their fears and anxieties, their hopes and dreams, their angsts and unfulfilled needs, their ever-so-human regrets and fears, and their enduring failures, without incurring judgment or being reprimanded. This requires active listening, confidentiality, and a willingness to demonstrate genuine care for their employees' well-being and success.

We also have to model and encourage open, honest communication by asking powerful questions, giving feedback, and making time for dialogue and reflection. These activities help leaders express their thoughts and feelings clearly and assertively, while also learning to listen actively and empathetically to others. We can support leaders to view setbacks less as failures and more as opportunities for learning and development. Having leaders share personal stories with one another is a way to communicate that failure is inevitable, even for the most successful. The best leaders dust it off, reframe the situation, and start again. Supporting the development of a growth mindset, where skills and abilities can be developed through effort and practice, is key to creating that psychologically safe environment.

Finally, it's necessary to provide leaders with the support and resources they need to be bold—to step into the unknown and out of their comfort zone. This might include guidance on decision-making, connecting with a mentor or peer-support team, or recommending them training or development opportunities. Knowing that they have a strong support system can help them feel more confident and secure in taking bold action. And perhaps the most exciting aspect of leadership coaching is the possibility we create for the leader and the organization in the long-term. Developing a growth mindset creates an organization where change becomes a possibility—where leaders are better prepared to deal with today's challenges, and are equipped for the changing business landscape they will have to navigate.

Leadership-Coaching Techniques

As a performance coach, I have a whole repertoire of techniques that I can tap into to help leaders level up their game. There's no one-size-fits-all approach. You always have to match the technique to the individual leader's needs and goals.

First up is active listening. This is the core of any good coaching relationship. It's not uncommon to get distracted while somebody is talking to you—maybe you're thinking of dinner or your next email. But not me! When a person who's hired me to coach them speaks, I'm listening hard. I'm trying to discern where this person is coming from, what makes them tick, and what's holding them back. When you're really listening to someone, listening at that electric moment when they reveal a formative truth about themselves, your relationship changes; it deepens in a way that is essential for any kind of performance coaching to work.

Listening is, of course, paramount; however, powerful questioning is also crucial. The questions I like to use with leaders are not your run-of-the-mill, check-the-box variety. I steer clear of yes-or-no questions. Instead, I ask ones that provoke powerful responses—that lead to seeing new possibilities, to challenging assumptions, to discoveries. "Huh, I never thought of it that way" kinds of responses.

Of course, questioning is great, but still, at some point, you have to get on with it. Start doing it. That's where feedback and reflection come in. I always make sure to give leaders honest, strong feedback on what they are doing right, and what could undergo change. Yet, it's only when I get them to reflect on their feedback that real change occurs. It's like when I hold up a mirror and say: "Look at you. What do you see?" It is then, when leaders can internally reflect on their experience, that they truly take forward the changes.

But keep in mind that growth isn't just about navel-gazing.

It's also about taking action. This is why I always ask leaders to make their goals, and action plans, sharply defined and achievement oriented. We agree to make a series of stops along the growth journey; we know where we are starting, we know where we are trying to end up, and, most of all, we have mapped out the stops, and the directions for each stop. There is nothing better than watching a leader tick off those boxes!

So now you're thinking: *That all sounds well and good, but just how would I actually go about learning to do any of this myself?* Well, just like test-driving a car before you buy it, role-playing and simulations can be your best friend—they are basically the scrimmages of leadership development.

For example, you can simulate and practice complex reorganization situations through structured role-playing exercises with fictional characters and scenarios. Participants obtain confidential role cards that detail their backgrounds and objectives. In their individual roles, they can try various communication methods and conflict-resolution techniques in a consequence-free setting.

Leaders benefit from such exercises because they offer a secure environment to learn through error while receiving prompt feedback and gaining essential social-emotional skills needed for real-life, high-pressure team situations. These exercises allow participants to develop genuine skills through creative problem-solving in a safe environment, free of consequence.

⩘

Leader-Specific Feedback Techniques

While the fundamental principles of feedback discussed in chapter III apply broadly, leaders face unique challenges that require specialized feedback approaches. Let's explore several feedback techniques tailored specifically for leadership development.

First, you can consider multi-rater feedback for leaders, which collects feedback from multiple sources and provides a panoramic view of a leader's impact across the organization. Take, for instance, a senior manager at a tech firm who received 360-degree feedback revealing that, while her superiors praised her strategic thinking, her subordinates felt she didn't communicate the company's vision effectively. This insight allowed her to focus on improving her communication skills, particularly in translating high-level strategy into actionable goals for her team.

Then, you have feedforward. This future-focused technique shifts the conversation from past performance to future improvements, aligning well with a leader's role in driving organizational progress. For example: Instead of dwelling on past miscommunications, a team leader can ask each team member, "What are two things I could do to communicate more effectively in our upcoming project?" This approach can generate practical suggestions and fosters a positive, solution-oriented team dynamic.

Adaptive-leadership feedback is also a great technique to assess a leader's ability to adapt their style to different situations and team members' developmental needs. I remember coaching a new department head who received feedback on his leadership flexibility. He learned that while he excelled at directing newer team members, he needed to adopt a more delegatory approach with his experienced staff to foster their autonomy and growth.

For senior leaders, feedback on their strategic acumen is equally valuable. I worked with a young CEO and provided him with specific feedback on his decision-making process during a recent market expansion. The feedback highlighted his strengths in data analysis, yet, it also suggested he could improve by seeking more diverse perspectives before finalizing major decisions.

Keep in mind that leadership effectiveness is also closely tied to emotional intelligence. Feedback in this area focuses on self-awareness, self-regulation, motivation, empathy, and social skills. For example, through EI-focused feedback, a project manager could discover that while she excels at self-motivation, she may need to improve her empathy. She could therefore learn to pay more attention to her team members' nonverbal cues and emotional states, possibly leading to improved team morale and productivity.

And let's not forget about conflict-resolution feedback. Leaders often serve as mediators, making conflict-resolution feedback vital. I recently worked with a department supervisor and witnessed firsthand how he handled a dispute between two team members. I praised his impartiality. However, I suggested he could improve by helping the parties find a mutually beneficial solution rather than simply ending the argument.

Lastly, you should not dismiss the value of vision and inspiration feedback, as a leader's ability to articulate and inspire others toward a vision is fundamental to their success. I once worked with an entrepreneur struggling to get much commitment from team members. After spending a few days meeting her team and getting a clearer understanding of the situation, I provided her with some feedback focusing on the fact that while her vision for the company was compelling, she needed to communicate it more frequently and connect it more clearly to day-to-day operations. By doing so, she significantly improved employee engagement and alignment with company goals.

By incorporating these leader-specific feedback techniques into your coaching practice, you can provide more targeted and impactful support to leaders at all levels. When you're working with emerging leaders, it's all about building those foundational skills and developing their competencies. With mid-level managers, you might focus more on decision-making and team dynamics. And when you're coaching senior executives, it's all about strategic thinking and driving organizational change.

And don't forget that leadership development isn't a solo journey. Which is why I'm a huge advocate for mentoring and peer coaching. A more seasoned mentor in your collaborator's corner (or a group of peers they can spar with) can be a literal game changer, this mentor or group cheering for them and offering sage advice when they take a wrong turn down a blind alley.

But here's the most important thing to remember: Coaching is ultimately about your employees. It's about their context, their agenda, and their outcomes. So, if they reckon they're good enough to take their leadership to the next level, then find them a performance coach who's good enough to understand them, listen to them, and help them soar.

While individual leadership is crucial, organizational success often hinges on effective teamwork. Building on our discussion of leadership coaching, we'll next examine how to apply coaching principles to enhance team dynamics and collaboration.

CHAPTER V

Team Dynamics and Collaboration

Opening Case: Strengthening Team Collaboration and Innovation

Consider a technology company in China struggling with poor team collaboration and communication, negatively impacting their innovation efforts. The company initiates a team coaching program to address these challenges. The coaches conduct an initial team assessment to discover the existing dynamics and sources of communication challenges, prior to launching a series of workshops designed to boost trust, communication, and collaborative problem-solving among the team.

Team-building exercises—in-house and virtual—and regular group coaching sessions to learn from real-time challenges and reinforce collaborative practices help to create bonds between teams and improve understanding. In addition, ongoing feedback exchange through regular, short check-ins or surveys ensure that communication remains open and that collaborative efforts continue to grow. The result is a dramatic decrease in the number of misunderstandings and actual conflicts among team members. Interactions become more open, and people feel more comfortable sharing ideas and supporting one another.

As a consequence, there's a rise in creative efforts, and more projects are successfully completed. The result? Much happier employees, and a much more pleasant work environment.

⋀

The Importance of Team Dynamics and Collaboration

As performance coaches, we can help teams fulfill their potential contribution to the organization's bottom line. We do this by fostering effective team dynamics and collaboration skills that can take a group from average to extraordinary.

The teams we coach have to rely on open communication and seamless collaboration. Sharing ideas, surfacing and solving problems, and generally working to achieve common objectives. We, coaches, need to create those conditions. We should encourage teams and their members to get rid of the silos that inhibit sharing and give them the freedom to flow information where needed.

However, that kind of harmony doesn't happen overnight, and it won't if team members aren't given a chance to trust each other and demonstrate respect toward one another. This is where we come in to apply the trust-building principles, discussed in chapter IV, to team settings. Our job is to create an atmosphere where every team member feels valued and appreciated. When we do that, we'll start to see individuals thrive and contribute their best.

But because teams are diverse, we must use—and not only leverage—a variety of different perspectives and skills. As facilitators of growth, it's our job to show teams how to use each member's strengths. It's like we're helping teams see how all of the puzzle pieces fit together. When those Tetris blocks come together, teams will think more creatively and make smarter decisions. And when teams learn to embrace and see their diversity as a strength, their work together becomes cohesive and streamlined.

But our role doesn't stop there. We also need to be the ones helping teams navigate the challenges of problem-solving and decision-making. By coaching them on how to analyze issues effectively, craft thought-out solutions, and make informed choices, we're setting them up for success. And when we see them starting to coordinate their efforts smoothly, share resources intelligently, and support each other wholeheartedly, that's when we know we're making a real impact on their productivity and efficiency.

And this is where it gets really exciting: By building teams that are robust and dynamic, we're not just helping them work better together. We're also nurturing a positive work culture that can shape an entire organization, positioning "busy-ness" and negativity in one place, and engagement, motivation, and commitment in another. We're essentially creating a ripple effect of positivity that can drive a company to new heights.

So, let's step up to the plate and be the team-dynamics champions our organizations need. Let's help these teams build unshakable trust, tap into their mix of superpowers, and enjoy that sense of team synchronicity—which we call collaborative flow. And most importantly, let's celebrate their wins along the way! Because when we do see a team performing consistently, we're reminded of just how powerful and impactful it can be.

And to all of the organizations out there: When it comes to the teams you support now (or are considering supporting), it's time to call performance coaches. We'll make your teams better. We'll help them become the best they can be. We'll push them to pursue big goals. Then, we'll celebrate right along with them when they conquer them.

The Role of Communication in Team Dynamics

We've got a critical role to play in helping teams master the art of communication. As coaches, it's our job to guide teams toward effective collaboration and goal achievement, and communication is the key that unlocks that potential.

First and foremost, we must be the messengers of transparency; we must coach teams about sharing information appropriately and with integrity. In doing so, we help to lay the groundwork of trust, which, when members feel informed and consulted about the reasoning behind decisions, will feel like rocket fuel for their team flow. We must encourage inclusion and responsiveness between members in order to keep teams glued together.

When we teach teams to be present, attentive, curious, and respond to each other's input—using their active listening skills—we create an environment where every voice is valued. Every voice is a critical instrument in the team orchestra. If we let each instrument shine, we can expect a great symphony of understanding. And if we help our team members feel heard, we can trust that they too will learn to listen.

Now, let's talk about feedback. Our job is to create a culture where feedback is seen as a gift, not a threat. While the fundamental principles of feedback discussed in chapter III also apply to teams, collective entities require specialized approaches to foster growth and collaboration. Let's explore feedback techniques tailored specifically for team development, building upon our earlier discussion of individual feedback.

After-action reviews[8] (AARs) are a very effective practice that offer a structured approach to team learning and continuous

---

[8] After-Action Reviews were first formalized and used by the US Army in the 1970s as a structured process to evaluate what happened, why it happened, and how to improve future outcomes after a mission or training exercise.

improvement. Unlike regular feedback, which typically focuses on individual development and performance over time, AARs engage the entire team in examining a specific event or project, identifying systemic issues, and capturing organizational learning. The last time I facilitated one of these was for a marketing team, following a challenging product launch. The team discovered that while their creative strategy was strong, they had underestimated the time needed for regulatory approvals. This insight led to more realistic timeline planning in future campaigns, improving overall project management.

Team performance dashboards are also great tools to visually represent the key team metrics and provide real-time collective feedback. For example, let's say a customer-service team implements a live dashboard displaying average response times, customer-satisfaction scores, and ticket-resolution rates. In turn, this visual feedback helps motivate the team to collaborate on improving their metrics, resulting in a 20 percent increase in customer satisfaction over three months.

Peer-to-peer feedback is equally valuable, as it offers structured opportunities for team members to provide feedback to each other, which in turn is great to foster open communication and mutual growth. For instance, take a consulting firm introducing monthly peer feedback sessions. During these, consultants share observations about each other's client interactions. This practice has the potential to not only improve individual performance but also strengthen team bonds and knowledge sharing.

Another simple yet highly effective framework I like to use is Start-Stop-Continue feedback. It encourages team members to reflect on behaviors and practices that should be introduced, discontinued, or maintained. For instance, a sales team implements monthly Start-Stop-Continue sessions. Through this process, they decided to start weekly skill-sharing meetings, stop sending repetitive internal emails, and continue their successful client follow-up protocol. These changes lead to improved team efficiency and knowledge sharing.

Finally, team-climate surveys are also very effective as a basis for team feedback. They involve regular assessments that provide insights into team morale, engagement, and perceived effectiveness. A few years ago, I worked with an HR team to implement quarterly climate surveys in their organization. These surveys revealed fluctuations in team morale correlating with project cycles. In response, we introduced "recharge weeks" between major projects, leading to sustained high engagement and reduced burnout. These "recharge weeks" focused on reduced workload to catch up on admin tasks, participation in skills-development workshops, out-of-office team-building activities, and an emphasis on wellness, with invited massage therapists and yoga sessions.

These diverse feedback techniques offer a comprehensive tool kit for team development. While each method has its strengths, the real power comes from integrating multiple approaches. For instance, you might use team-climate surveys to identify broad areas of concern, then apply peer-to-peer feedback to build on team strengths, and finally use Start-Stop-Continue feedback to define specific action steps. By incorporating these team-specific feedback techniques into your coaching practice, you can provide more targeted support for collective growth and performance improvement.

But what happens when the road gets bumpy? It's here that our conflict-resolution skills get tested. As coaches, we need to guide teams in dealing with issues head-on and diplomatically. It's like we're the mediators, helping teams navigate tough conversations and come out stronger on the other side. When we coach teams to resolve such conflicts in a way that brings them closer together as a group, they're much better set up in the long run.

And finally, let's not forget the power of inclusive participation. As performance coaches, we can ensure that the seats around the table are full with every member of the team. When we ask teams to consider the various lenses through which they see their issues, we activate a goldmine of innovation and better decision-making. We set free much-needed ingenuity, insight, and, yes, smarter decisions as we tap into the insight of their diverse members. In order for any group of individuals to bond as a team, we want to create that shared feeling that they're all in it together.

As coaches, one of our greatest opportunities is to help teams forge unbreakable bonds of belonging and commitment. We achieve this by asking teams to see themselves as actors in a vision and mission, not just as autonomous individuals. The space we're attempting to fill, the interstice we're trying to serve, is all about encouraging teams to see themselves as a tapestry, a collective entity woven from many threads and brought into equilibrium when the members collectively share the loads and pressures. The best we can do, you and me, is to foster the kind of connectedness that enables teams to move mountains together.

Strategies for Building High-Performing Teams

We all know that building a knockout team doesn't happen by accident. It takes some serious strategy and a whole lot of heart. So, take heart—because I'm going to give you a couple of proven techniques that will have your team dynamics skyrocketing, and your collaboration at new heights.

First, we have goals. It's important to set an ambitious bar and ensure that everyone who joins the team knows exactly what they're pulling for. People can't pull forth something they aren't privy to. So set aside some time to map out those goals with your team.

And, as always, goals are just the beginning. If you want to have a team that can really pull together efficiently, then you're going to need to lower the barriers; get everyone out from behind their silos and open up those lines of communication! I'm talking about a place where everyone feels absolutely safe to share, to speak freely, to even (shock, horror) give some feedback. It's scary to put yourself out there, but when your team isn't afraid of the hard conversations, that's when you really soar. Schedule some regular check-ins. Maybe a session here and a feedback loop there.

Now, let's talk about the element that binds all these great teams together and makes them so effective: trust and respect. You can't just snap your fingers and make these appear, but you can definitely set the stage. It starts with you, coach. Model those behaviors and show your team what it looks like to have each other's backs. My favorite way to jump-start this process is to get a little creative. Team-building activities and social events are like trust and respect boot camps, or whatever you want to call them. These opportunities to team build—to lower the collective guard, to get silly, or in some way just to get to know each other as humans instead of coworkers—go a long way toward promoting social connectedness. Many of these team-building exercises can be modified for virtual environments, as discussed in chapter IX.

But the reality is that building a dream team isn't just about singing "Kumbaya" and doing trust falls. It's also about embracing the things that make each person unique. So, you have to respect those differences among people—you need diversity and inclusion! Diversity and inclusion are what high-performing teams run on. Value this melting pot you have of perspectives and experiences and skills. It's a pot of gold. And it's also what drives innovation.

Of course, even the best teams have their rough patches sometimes. Conflicts happen, and that's okay! The key is to have a game plan for when they do. Just be ready for it. Make sure your team has some serious conflict-resolution skills at its disposal. Active listening, empathy, problem-solving, prosocial mojo—the whole shebang. And don't forget to give them some rules of the road, like how they should commit to resolving sticky situations. When your team knows they've got the tools and the support to work through tough times, they'll be unstoppable.

However, keep in mind that tools and skills are necessary, but not sufficient for winning the game. Who does what is just as important as who's responsible for what. That means crystal-clear roles and responsibilities. Think of a game of football—individual players are positioned and assigned responsibilities and how they're accountable for the team's success. You'll avoid a lot of confusion when the game starts if you take the time to spell it all out now, ensuring everyone is on the same page.

Now, even the greatest team can't win if they don't have the right equipment. When guiding your employees, you need to be providing your team access to the right training, tools, and tech needed to annihilate. And don't just play that one song. Learning and growing is a continuous process. Never stop learning new tricks or best practices and, more importantly, never stop making the people around you strong enough to crush it alongside you. Invest in them, and they'll reciprocate with more wins than ever before.

But what makes a team really unbeatable is that seismic sense of camaraderie that comes from feeling that you're more than a bunch of disconnected employees. That sense that you're not just a bunch of individuals clocking in and out, but a true unit, a family even. Foster that team spirit by celebrating every win, big or small. Shout out those individual contributions and make sure everyone knows how much they matter. And have some fun in the process! If your team is having fun and getting along, there's nothing they can't accomplish.

In this chapter, we emphasized the significant influence of team dynamics on employee engagement and retention. In the next chapter, we'll explore how performance coaching can be leveraged to boost engagement, improve job satisfaction, and retain top talent.

CHAPTER VI

Employee Engagement and Retention

Opening Case: Enhancing Employee Engagement and Reducing Turnover

Consider an automaker in Germany experiencing very high turnover and low employee engagement, which is negatively affecting customer service and overall sales performance. As a result, the company initiates a broad engagement and retention strategy. First, they roll out an engagement survey to capture employees' opinions on what is working well and where they feel improvements could be made. They also initiate a formal recognition program so that they can celebrate employees' individual effort and contribution more regularly.

Professional-development opportunities are offered, including workshops, training programs, and career-advancement pathways. Coaches work individually with employees to come up with tailored development plans related to specific performance goals and career-path objectives. Regular check-ins between employees and managers take place to evaluate the employees' progress, provide ongoing feedback, or address concerns. This increases the level of employee engagement, with employees reporting that they feel valued, motivated, and committed to the organization. Turnover rates drop as employees feel more committed to the organization and see clear career-development opportunities. Enhanced employee engagement leads to better customer interactions and higher satisfaction scores, resulting in improved sales performance and overall business growth.

The Importance of Employee Engagement and Retention

As performance coaches, it's our mission to create a workplace culture in which team members are inspired, engaged, and willing to bring their whole selves to work each day. When you've got a workforce of engaged employees, they will stop an impending disaster in its tracks and embrace the climb to the top of the corporate ladder like there's no tomorrow.

I'll never forget one of my first coaching assignments. I walked into the Yangon[9] office of a large international, public organization—slightly naively and armed with my shiny new tool kit—prepared to transform lives left, right, and center. Intriguingly, it didn't take me long to discover that not everyone shared my fervor. The quiet majority was "just doing their time"— punctual enough to clock in, do their hours, then clock out to live their real lives later in the evening. And then there were the stars—the minority who turned up early to tackle their newest projects, stayed late to put out fires, who put their heart and soul into their work. The engaged ones. And yes, this minority was the driving force behind that organization's success.

So, what's the secret recipe for building a team of engaged superstars? For starters, engaged employees are productivity powerhouses. When you've got people who are truly passionate about what they do, they're not just meeting expectations.

---

[9] The former capital city of Myanmar (formerly known as Burma)

They embody the concept of excellence because they refuse to do anything less. And that translates to some serious ROI for your organization.

Yet, it's not just about the bottom line. Engaged employees are also the culture champions of your company. The highly contagious passion they display will permeate throughout your business and establish a culture that will attract more top talent like them. Potential A-players tend to be inspired by the presence of other A-players. The more engaged employees you have, the more A-players you'll attract and retain in your business.

And let's talk about the financial impact. Think about how expensive it is to replace a star performer. You're talking about a huge investment of time and money—from recruitment to training and onboarding a single new hire. Whereas if you have energized employees who are all on the same page and committed to your team, you can avoid the cost of turnover and garner all their great institutional knowledge and wisdom.

But perhaps the most remarkable thing about engaged employees is how they relate to your clients and customers. There's nothing better than working with people who are strongly committed to your company's mission, and who show their passion for providing quality service. You can feel it. They foster "wow" moments, and clients sense the authenticity. That is what inspires true and lasting brand loyalty that keeps clients coming back for more.

And finally, you have innovation. To be a leading company, you need people who are constantly striving for better ways to work. Engaged employees are the ones who keep the light bulbs alight; who always seek opportunities to improve processes, products, or performance; and who can outpace the competition.

So, what's our action plan here? How do we cultivate a workforce of engaged rock stars? The solution is to develop a culture of purpose and growth; a culture of genuine recognition.

We need to align employees to the organizational vision and mission, support them to develop and grow, and celebrate individual success. It's essential to make organizations antifragmented places of work that promote psychological safety, trust, and interpersonal relationships, built on an exchange of honest information and authentic dialogue that assumes the best of others.

And most importantly, we need to lead by example. We set the pace for everyone in the organization to follow. We need to have the fire in our belly, and we need to have the commitment, the desire to win, to be the tip of the spear, to deliver and to enable breakthrough—the fangs of the weapon. It's necessary to be the coaches that our people want to listen to, want to learn from, want to grow with, and want to be transformed by.

Strategies for Enhancing Employee Engagement

So, let's explore how we can help organizations supercharge their employee engagement and create a workforce that's fired up and ready to take on the world.

I have worked with many organizations as a coach or consultant and know that, to drive engagement, it's vital to understand what is most important to employees. With an environment that values, motivates, and commits to everyone, anything is possible.

Most importantly, employee engagement is about giving individuals more meaning and purpose in their jobs. Time and again, I encourage my clients to connect their team's work responsibilities to their personal values and goals. When they do, engagement goes through the roof. No longer just "a job", their work becomes "a calling."

For starters, it needs to be evident to individual employees exactly how their role fits in with those wider organizational goals. The more that employees see a connection—even if not always directly measurable—between the purpose of the organization, or what it stands for, and their day-to-day role, and one that is meaningful to them, the more engaged they will be. It's our job to help organizations connect those dots and make work meaningful.

And the two Rs of recognition and reward are also important. I believe that recognition impacts direct, on-the-job behaviors through the power of praise. Celebrating wins and successes big and small, from individual achievements to team milestones, personalizes and humanizes the company's priorities, and can be rocket fuel for motivation—a little goes a long way.

But we can't stop there. We also have to provide opportunities to invest in employees for the long haul: training, skill building, and planning for career growth all contribute to helping employees feel appreciated, noticed, and valued. This makes them more likely to stay and give it their all.

None of this occurs without strong leadership, of course. As facilitators of professional growth, our job is to help leaders inspire, enable, and guide their teams; to spur people to speak up; and to create a positive climate in their organizations. Psychological safety plays a crucial role in engagement by enabling employees to feel like leaders have their backs.

And let's not forget about work-life balance. In the mad world we live in, flexibility matters. What can we do to help keep organizations as productive and relevant as possible? Well, let's start by adding more flexibility—from telecommuting to extending weekend hours in the office so that employees can find ways to juggle their obligations inside and outside of work. After all, research shows that happier, more engaged people are those who report having healthier work-life balance.

Creating a strong work culture is important for employee

engagement too. As coaches we need to contribute to helping organizations build respectful, open, and collaborative cultures. When employees experience a workplace in which they feel comfortable and supported, they're free to bring their best selves to the table.

Lastly, empowerment. If you delegate decision-making and you trust your employees, great things will happen. They will become "intrapreneurs," innovating and contributing in ways you couldn't even imagine. We are in the business of helping organizations become more empowering and, thus, helping employees bring out their best.

The Role of Performance Coaching in Engagement and Retention

Performance coaching can enhance employee engagement and retention because it has the personalized support, guidance, and development opportunities that employees seek. And let me tell you, this level of support isn't just a nice-to-have—it's absolutely essential for employees' growth and satisfaction at work.

I remember one of my very first truly performance-oriented coaching assignments. It was with a struggling employee who found herself at a current onslaught of circumstances, issues, and expectations that were proving to be far more than she could manage. She was relatively young but very capable and, with some polishing, showed promising potential. On the other hand, she was completely checked out, disengaged, frustrated, and already had her mind made up to leave. Nonetheless, she still agreed to meet with me. We began our work, and after several months the light finally started to flicker on. We went deep into what made her tick—what she cared about, what she was trying to achieve and accomplish. Together, we crafted a development plan that was unique, just for her.

That's the essence of performance coaching—individualized development plans that are tailored to an employee's specific career aspirations. If we make employees feel like they're doing something that matters for the company that employs them, if we ensure that employees feel like we value them enough to see them as whole people, for whom we validate specific growth needs, we can make it that much easier for them to visualize themselves in their own future working with us.

As performance coaches, we play a crucial role in providing regular feedback and support. We help employees recognize their strengths and identify areas for improvement. This continuous feedback loop, as discussed earlier, plays a crucial role in keeping employees engaged and motivated, clearly demonstrating the company's commitment to their ongoing success.

However, feedback isn't the only thing that coaching offers. It's very much a skill-development process. Performance coaching means investing in the skills and competencies that employees need to do their jobs well. As a result, they stick around.

Career development is another crucial area where performance coaching can help enormously. If employees feel they are faced with a dead-end job and have no chance of developing further within the organization, they might start to look for new horizons, wherever they see them fit with their personal and professional aspirations. We can help employees identify and exploit career-development opportunities, encouraging them to identify and develop the skills they need in order to achieve their professional goals. This direction is also a huge motivator and will encourage greater retention as your employees advance.

Going back to my coaching story—it wasn't always easy. I recall committing to a biweekly schedule of check-ins, feedback, and a whole lot of encouragement. A couple of months in, I noticed this employee going from strength to strength. She was taking on new responsibilities, quickly learning new processes, and smiling more often too. A few months later, she was leading the charge on some exciting new projects and—come to think of it—she was a lot happier to come into the office now. A year after we put an end to our coaching relationship, I was contacted by her boss. After an incredible first six months on the floor, she'd had two upward promotions and was absolutely killing it in her current role. But more than that, she was happy, engaged, and invested. That's what performance coaching can do.

Performance coaching also helps employees gain confidence in themselves, and to develop their resilience to overcome adversity. Therefore, by raising confidence and developing their coping skills, people will commit to and remain dedicated to their roles; which, in our troubled times, is so valuable.

With such a platform in place, issues that may undermine morale, productivity, and motivation can be openly addressed and, in many cases, resolved before things take a turn for the worse. The side benefit is that this sort of work culture creates an environment where employees know their employers care about them—a powerful inducement to loyalty.

In today's crazy competitive job market, retention is everything. You can't afford to lose your top talent because they feel stuck or unappreciated. Consider performance coaching to be your secret turnover-prevention weapon. Performance coaching helps your employees feel supported, that you see who they truly are, and that you are willing to invest in them to succeed.

So, if you're not already making performance coaching a priority, what are you waiting for? Sure, it takes effort, commitment, and genuine care. But the dividends are huge and immediate. When employees feel supported, valued, and empowered to grow, they don't just stick around, they flourish. They innovate. They steer the enterprise forward in ways that you could never have predicted.

Measuring Employee Engagement and Retention

If you're a coach, or anyone else who works with organizations to drive performance, I can't stress this enough: Measure engagement and attrition every six months. I don't think any modern organization can afford to do without any longer. It's an absolute must-have if you want to create a workplace where people are happy, motivated, and in it for the long haul.

One of the first things I always recommend to my clients is to conduct employee surveys on a regular basis. And if you're thinking that a survey sounds boring, you're right. Yet they're also a performance coach's secret weapon. They are the easiest way to find out what's on people's minds (within reason), so you know where to start in bringing about meaningful change.

However, the power of surveys doesn't begin and end with them, per se. In my coaching practice, I always emphasize the importance of exit interviews to the sponsoring client. When someone decides they're not going to stay with you anymore, then they certainly aren't staying—but they're also not leaving empty-handed, or at least they shouldn't be. There's an envelope of free wisdom right there for the taking: What would it have taken to get them to stay? Is what they're describing a single, odd case, or does it point to a trend or systemic issue? And is there anything that you could have done differently in the long-term to prevent their leaving? These are the kinds of insights that can help you make some serious strides in your retention efforts.

Stay interviews are also important, and I usually strongly encourage my clients to sit down with their top performers and ask them what's making their experience so positive. What do they like about working here? What keeps them engaged on a day-to-day basis? What can the company do to improve their experience? That kind of open-book feedback from your most invested talent is an indication of what to replicate throughout your organization (more on that in chapter XV).

Yeah, yeah, all that sounds good, but what about the ROI? It's all well and good to understand the underlying motivations, but it's all about results. And you are right, at the end of the day—it's all about the bottom line. I always try reminding clients to also track more tangible outputs such as productivity, quality of work, or basic, quantifiable performance metrics. You have a much better chance of getting leadership buy-in if you can point to hard numbers that prove your engagement efforts are actually having a positive impact.

But engagement is only part of the picture. As a performance coach, one of my mantras is that "retention isn't optional." Why would you engage people just to have them walk out the door a few months down the line? That makes absolutely no sense to me. That's where retention comes in, where you start to track why people are leaving and where they're going. If you're monitoring your retention—looking at traps to success and tracking the turnover patterns and trends—then you can start to make adjustments to your strategy.

Pulse surveys serve that purpose well and are a wonderful tool on a performance coach's shelf. If you need to know right then how employees are feeling, send a pulse survey for data that will help you identify whether any course correction is needed right away. It's all about being agile and responsive to your employees' needs (more on pulse surveys in chapter XV).

And, finally, never underestimate a good old-fashioned focus group. When you bring a group of employees together to really dive deep on a specific topic related to engagement or retention, magic can happen. You'll walk away with insights and solutions you may never have uncovered through a survey or an interview. And don't be afraid to integrate technology to support these efforts. Technology-driven engagement surveys and pulse checks, explored further in chapter XIII, allow for more regular and granular insights into employee sentiment.

Engaged employees are better equipped to handle organizational changes. As we move forward, we'll discuss how coaching can play a vital role in supporting individuals and teams through periods of transformation.

CHAPTER VII

Supporting Organizational Change

Opening Case: Facilitating Smooth Organizational Change

A manufacturing company in the US is going through a major organizational transformation to adopt new technologies and processes and is using a structured change-management coaching program to support the effort. Leaders in the company are trained in change-management principles and strategies, and then paired with coaches who work with them one-on-one to develop the skills they would need to help their teams through the change.

A comprehensive communication plan is designed to inform and guide all employees on the changes happening and how they affect them. Workshops are created to train the employees on new technological and process changes. Reverse feedback processes are created to get input from the employees on the change implementation and to modify the change-management program accordingly. As a result, the company effectively upgrades its technological and process changes without a production halt. Leaders grow more skillful in their change management and become more confident and competent. The employees quickly adapt to the technology and processes, leading to improved efficiency and productivity. The feedback we receive is overwhelmingly positive, and employees report feeling supported through the change.

The Importance of Change Management

If I'm supporting a client dealing with a significant change, I always aim to help them see it as an opportunity rather than a problem, and I recognize that the space in which to do that can be profoundly difficult to pinpoint.

I always start by having them get very clear about their goals and priorities: What do they want to accomplish? What does their future vision of success look like? Once we have that North Star, so to speak, a plan can be devised, and we can start mapping our way there.

A big part of that plan always involves communication: We have to remind ourselves how important it is to keep our people in the loop, and how much it means to people when they feel that they're heard. This means being willing to talk about what we're going to change, why we're changing it, and what that means for our employees. It means creating forums that offer the opportunity for openness, for people to tell you unvarnished truths (whether or not that's really what you want to hear).

But creating buy-in is never enough. To create lasting change, action needs to follow words, and performance coaching provides the structure for just that. Together with my clients, I identify the capabilities and behaviors they need to enable them to achieve success, and we carve out a road map to get there. This might involve training or mentoring programs, or even getting employees out on the "shop floor" to get their hands dirty—whatever it takes to build those new muscles.

And no change effort is complete without celebrating

the wins. As facilitators of professional growth, we have to understand that, often, during the middle of the change effort, people get caught up in the day-to-day. They continue to struggle with execution. The excitement at the beginning of change can wear off, and employees can become discouraged. It often helps to take a step back and recognize the positive signs of progress.

So, if you're a coach responsible for supporting people through a big transition, my advice is this: Change is a process, not a destination; it takes time, it takes talent, and it takes patience. And if your employees are armed with the right mindset, and have access to the right support, then they can come out the other side better prepared for whatever life throws at them next.

Key Principles of Effective Change Management

If you want your employees to excel at navigating change, you'll need to understand and have at the ready some key principles. These aren't just fluff—they're the real deal, the secret sauce to making change stick for the long haul.

First, you've got to make sure your employees know the vision and the objectives, and are very clear on both. If they don't know where they're going, how can you expect them to get there?

I once worked with a client company in the middle of implementing a new customer-service strategy. They had all these grandiose ideas; still, when I asked them to spell out exactly what success looked like, they could not phrase it clearly. So, we sat down and hammered out a clear vision, with measurable goals and a timeline. And guess what? Once everyone knew what they were working toward, the whole team rallied around it like it was their new religion.

But vision alone isn't enough—you need strong leadership

to steer the ship. And I'm not limiting this to suits at the top. As the coach, you are helping leaders at every level step up and lead the change. Or, to put it another way, you're helping them be more directive, more supportive, and—good gracious—more of a cheerleader than they've probably been since their school days. Leading change is hard work, and those doing the leading better know it right from the outset that you've got their back.

I once worked with a manager who was trying to implement new processes and found that his team wasn't having any of it. He was getting frustrated and ready to throw in the towel. But we worked together to help him talk about why this change was right for them, and to engage his team and show he was right there with them in the trenches, too. And guess what? It was these small extra efforts that made a difference. His team went from dragging their feet to being the biggest advocates for change in the company.

You can't just impose change from on high and expect everyone to fall in line. You've got to engage stakeholders at every level, from the front line to the C-suite. You have to stay on the front line, you have to be in the C-suite, you have to go into every function, every level, and say: "What are you guys facing? Here's what I see. These are the challenges I have. Let's figure out how to do this so we all optimize our efficiency." If people feel like it's something they have a voice in, they are going to go along with you.

Perhaps the most difficult challenge in change management is resistance from employees who feel threatened by a change effort and thus push back against new initiatives. Our role as coaches is to help leaders anticipate and overcome resistance by fostering proactive communication, addressing concerns head-on, and helping employees develop the skills and mindset necessary to embrace change. I once had a client who was trying to roll out a new software system, but they were getting a ton of pushback from their employees. They held a number of focus groups and surveys to solicit feedback and suggestions, and the upshot of it was that a lot of fear was feeding the resistance. Employees worried the new system would make their jobs harder or even make some of their positions redundant. By giving them a voice—empowering them and including them in the process—we found that we could defuse this fear and get people excited about what was possible.

Of course, none of this happens without clear communication. Poor communication can derail the best-laid plans if employees do not know why change is happening, when the process will begin and end, or what the results will look like. You're not going to drop a bomb, walk out of the room, and then expect people to figure it out for themselves. The coach's role is to help leaders communicate early, often, and absolutely transparently. That means regular updates, Q&A sessions, and a willingness to have tough conversations when needed.

I once worked with an organization going through a merger that was buzzing with rumors. People started fleeing what they thought was an inevitable sinking boat. However, we worked with the leadership team to develop a plan for what, how, and when to communicate, even if there wasn't much new information to spread. And you know what? Just that little bit of extra effort went a long way in calming people's fears and keeping them engaged.

But communication isn't just about talking—that's only half the recipe for an effective change implementation. The rest of the recipe involves the training and support to help employees build the literacies they need to prosper in the new world as envisioned in the change agenda. As a performance coach, this is where you really cut your teeth. This is where you really get to play the part of the change agent. And that's because the biggest job you've got is figuring out what people lack and how to provide what they're lacking. If it takes a formal training program, an on-the-job coach, or a shoulder to cry on, at the end of the day your job as a change agent is really about making sure people have what they need.

A while back I worked with a sales team that was struggling to adapt to a new CRM (customer-relationship management) system. They were frustrated, confused, and literally close to mutiny, but a full-bodied training program with plenty of learning, hands-on practice, and one-on-one support meant that, within a few weeks, they were using the system as though they'd been born into it.

More importantly, it's crucial to note that change is never a one-and-done deal. It's a process, and one you need to be on top of all the time, course correcting on the fly. It's your job as a coach to help the employee remain engaged with the data, get feedback, and make corrections to stay on track. Because even the best-laid plans can go awry, and the secret is not being stuck on the preplanned ride. So, always stay flexible and adaptable.

The Role of Performance Coaching in Change Management

As a performance coach, I've seen firsthand how transformative coaching can be when organizations are navigating change. It's our job to equip leaders and employees with the skills, mindset, and resilience they need to not just survive transitions, but to thrive in them.

One of the key things we should focus on is developing leadership qualities. It's essential to work closely with leaders to strengthen their strategic thinking and ability to communicate and inspire a team. And let me tell you, when leaders have these skills in their tool kit, they're able to guide their teams through change with a level of confidence and ease that's truly impressive.

Leaders will experience stress and pressure while driving change, and they will require support. They will need access to tangible strategies to handle those stressors. Helping them build a resilient mind will improve focus, productivity, and engagement, and can make a world of difference to how the change journey goes.

Effective communication is another of the key areas that is critical to focus on in performance coaching. We should support leaders to craft a vision and articulate the objectives and value of the change in ways that are easily understood and compelling. The clearer the communication, the less reason people have to move into a state of resistance, becoming disengaged from the value of the change.

Then you have problem-solving. It's another important area where we need to provide a lot of support. We should work with leaders and teams to tackle any issues that arise during the change process. It's all about being proactive! By helping teams with problem-solving, we can keep the initiative on track and throw in yet another dose of confidence and sense of control that's so vital for team members.

Encouraging a growth mindset is also a critical part of our role, in that we can help employees reframe change as an opportunity for learning and development rather than a threat. This shift in perspective about what change means for them, and how they can benefit from it, can be a key lever in keeping employees engaged and energized.

Lastly, we must ensure individual goals align with the wider organizational goal of the change: As soon as people feel their output plays a part in the company's overall success, they will start to feel that investment. And that, in my experience, is one of the key drivers of successful change management.

Strategies for Effective Change Management

When organizations bring me in to help with change management, I am driven by one and only one goal, that is, to make the process as smooth and successful as possible. Over the years, I've developed a tool kit of strategies and tactics to make this happen, but there's one framework that I keep coming back to time and time again: the Prosci ADKAR[10] model.

When change is to happen, one of the first things we are expected to do is work with organizations to create a bulletproof change plan that is then the basis for everything else: to help them clearly articulate their vision and ambition; to identify compelling and motivating goals and milestones; and to articulate a timeline and all the critical steps it will take to get there. All of the communication, training, support, milestones, check-ins . . . everything gets tracked back to the change plan. Our job is to make sure no stone is left unturned and that there's a systematic approach in place.

I remember one project in particular where the ADKAR model was a real game changer. We were working with a company that was undergoing a rather significant digital transformation. Employees were very resistant due to understandable fears about the poorly communicated changes to come and the possible effects on their jobs. Using the ADKAR model as a reference point, we were easily able to break down the change process into digestible steps while also dealing with the resistance employees were experiencing.

The beauty of the ADKAR model is that it ensures that each of these five critical success factors are addressed (Awareness,

---

[10] The ADKAR® model (Awareness, Desire, Knowledge, Ability, Reinforcement) is a framework for change management developed by Prosci, Inc. ADKAR® is a registered trademark of Prosci, Inc.

Desire, Knowledge, Ability, Reinforcement) prior to, during, and after any change program.

In that digital transformation project, I just mentioned, we began by raising awareness of the reasons for change and the benefits to be gained. We then developed desire by showing what was in it for employees and how they might be able to contribute to the success of the program. We provided training and support to build knowledge and ability, and, finally, we celebrated milestones and successes along the way to reinforce the positive progress. And it all supported a successful transition.

Next, we should also develop engaged and equipped leaders, ready to drive change, at all levels. Tailored leadership training and performance coaching can give leaders the tools and confidence they need to successfully lead teams through change. Engaged leaders make a huge difference in the success of the initiative.

Communication is another big area where we should provide a lot of guidance. Regular, two-way communication to keep all interested parties informed is yet another key strategy. We can use a variety of channels to ensure the message gets through. We should always emphasize the importance of transparency in building trust and reducing resistance to change.

I'm also a big believer in the power of training and development during times of change. Take advantage of these opportunities to constantly train people to gain the skills and knowledge they need to succeed in the new environment. Personalized performance coaching can be especially impactful here, and it's one of my favorite tools for providing targeted support.

Creating a culture that supports change is another key factor. As coaches, we help organizations foster an environment that values flexibility, adaptability, and continuous improvement. We work on promoting collaboration and innovation. When you have a culture like this, it makes it so much easier for people to embrace change.

Throughout the change process, we should always keep a close eye on progress and help the organization stay agile. We gather regular input from stakeholders and use that feedback to make real-time adjustments as needed. This helps ensure we stay on track and can address any challenges that arise.

Finally, I'm sure you have realized by now that I am a huge proponent of celebrating milestones and successes along the way. It's necessary to encourage organizations to do this regularly. It reinforces the change in effect, it shows the benefits of the change in action, and it provides an opportunity for members to see the good things that the change brings as it happens, which helps keep motivations high and all employees committed to the transformation journey. Perhaps the biggest reason why most change initiatives fail is because they aren't followed up and reinforced. It's great to announce a change, but it also takes a lot of patient and positive reinforcement to ensure the new behavior and processes stick and become part of the culture.

Now, although this chapter refers to ADKAR—a holistic (and popular) change model—it's by no means the only change model an organization can implement.

In fact, one of the better-known models is Kotter's 8-Step Process[11]: a sequential model for change that includes: 1) creating a sense of urgency, 2) forming a guiding coalition, 3) developing a vision and strategy, 4) communicating the change vision, 5) empowering employees for action, 6) generating short-term wins, 7) consolidating gains and producing more change, and lastly, 8) anchoring new approaches in the culture.

Another such classic is Lewin's Change Management Model[12], composed of three stages: unfreeze, change, and refreeze. "Unfreeze" would be readying people and organizations

---

[11] Used with reference to Kotter's 8-Step Process for Leading Change: John P. Kotter, *Leading Change* (Harvard Business Review Press, 1996).

[12] Based on Kurt Lewin's Change Management Model, originally published in Field Theory in Social Science (1951).

for change—probably by building a sense of urgency and buy-in. "Change" would be the change itself, such as new behaviors, processes, or systems. And "refreeze" needs to be done to confirm that the change is happening and to establish the new normal.

Other examples include the McKinsey 7-S Framework[13] (where the concept of seven integral organizational factors—strategy, structure, systems, shared values, style, staff, and skills—are linked to one another), and the Bridges Transition Model[14] (that recognizes that transitions are emotional and psychological in nature, and attempt to account for the need for change support through accompanying employees through the three states of transition: ending, neutral zone, and new beginning).

All these models and approaches can be helpful for us as coaches to know about, because they all give us a different perspective on what we're trying to achieve with change management. If we know the key principles and strategies associated with each, and how and why each works, then we can more easily draw on the most appropriate of these models and adapt the approaches to suit the context and culture of the organizations we're working with. Ultimately, we want to develop leaders and employees with strong tool kits to manage change well going forward, drawing on the best elements of these various models, and calibrating them to the context and culture of the work.

Change management and diversity initiatives often go hand in hand. In the next chapter, we'll explore how coaching can promote diversity and inclusion, creating a more equitable and innovative workplace.

---

[13] Developed by Tom Peters and Robert Waterman during their tenure at McKinsey & Company. Thomas J. Peters and Robert H. Waterman Jr., *In Search of Excellence: Lessons from America's Best-Run Companies*, (Harper Business, 2006).

[14] The Bridges Transition Model, introduced by William Bridges in *Managing Transitions: Making the Most of Change* (Da Capo Press, 1991), focuses on the emotional and psychological aspects of transitioning through change.

CHAPTER VIII

Promoting Diversity and Inclusion

Opening Case: Fostering Diversity and Inclusion

Consider a US-based media company that feels the need, after an episode of bad press from social media, to increase diversity and inclusion among its teams as a lever for innovation and to appropriately reflect its customer base. The company decides to implement a comprehensive diversity and inclusion (D&I) strategy. Diversity training sessions are organized to raise awareness and educate employees on the importance of diversity and inclusion. Coaches are brought in to provide personalized support and development to diverse employee groups and help them navigate career challenges and achieve their goals.

With the establishment of employee resource groups (ERGs), the company offers a platform for employees to easily connect with each other, share their experiences, and provide mutual support. The company initiates a mentorship program for employees from underrepresented groups, and revisits existing company policies to ensure they are more inclusive and supportive of diversity, aligning better with the overall objectives of the transition. As a result, employees become more aware of diversity and inclusion issues and their importance to the organization. Underrepresented groups of employees feel more supported and valued, leading to higher engagement and job satisfaction. Retention rates improve, therefore enhancing organizational stability. The diverse and inclusive environment leads to more innovative ideas and solutions, contributing to the company's growth and success.

The Importance of Diversity and Inclusion

Finding ways to enhance D&I has become a critical priority for organizations willing to sustain a competitive advantage. Different people bring in different perspectives, different work and life experiences, and different ways to look at problems. A healthy workplace culture benefits from true diversity of thought, fostering a more innovative, energized, and productive environment. And so, we should commit to merit-based inclusion—ensuring qualified individuals have equal opportunities regardless of cultural background, ethnicity, sexual orientation, gender, or religion. This proper inclusion ensures that employees know they are valued, respected, and trusted, therefore able to give their best to the job.

Imagine this: You gather a bunch of people, put them together in a room, and get them all working side by side. They've come from all over, had all kinds of life experiences, held all kinds of different jobs, and tackled all sorts of problems with many different approaches. What do you end up with? You've got a culture that's dynamic, innovative, and incredibly productive. Indispensable, really.

But here's the thing—just having a diverse group of people isn't enough. It takes more than diversity of bodies to get there. And you need to be sure that all of those individuals know that they're welcome and, moreover, that they're needed and valued.

That's where the inclusion aspect comes in; once you create a culture in which each and every person feels empowered to do their best, that's when the sparks begin to fly.

And now for the why of diversity and inclusion. Diversity promotes creativity and innovation. A diverse team has diverse ways of looking at things, diverse experiences, and diverse capabilities—they have a greater ability to provide novel ideas or solutions to a problem than a team of people who think alike. And that's simply because everyone is looking at the problem through their own unique lens, which leads to a more well-rounded approach.

But that's not all—diverse teams also tend to make better decisions. When you've got a group with different viewpoints, they're more likely to consider a wider range of options and potential outcomes before making a call. Their exploration of a larger range of alternatives can actually lead to better decisions for the organization.

And let's not forget about employee engagement. People will stay if they feel like their unique contribution gives meaning to their project. They will stay if they feel cared for by the organization, as well as respected and acknowledged by their coworkers. When employees feel appreciated and supported, they're just more likely to stick around. Plain and simple.

And more still. Diversity enables companies to push the boundaries of talent. By expanding the number of people they seek out and welcome into their ranks, they gain access to talent they otherwise might have missed.

In addition to the skills and experiences these people bring, having a workforce that mirrors the diversity of a community allows organizations to distinguish themselves from their competitors. Diverse teams are better at serving a diverse client base. If your employees hail from a variety of backgrounds, they're likely to bring a wide perspective into the wants, needs, and experiences of different customer groups. This allows organizations to cater products, services, and messages to the reality of their customer base, and that leads to happier, more devoted clients.

Key Principles of Diversity and Inclusion

It's important to understand the key principles that make diversity & inclusion efforts really stick. It's not just about going through the motions—it's about creating lasting, impactful change. So, let's break down what you need to be focusing on in your coaching role.

For starters, you've got to make sure that the leadership team is fully committed to D&I. Their buy-in is essential, and you are the coach who gets them to see why and how. Ask them to demonstrate inclusive behaviors and embrace the challenge associated with the implementation. If the higher-ups are visible in their interest for the work, it's a big statement to the rest of the organization that you are setting D&I as a priority.

Next up, it's essential to help the organization create equal opportunities for everyone. And I mean for everyone. Remember, there might be employees who perceive diversity efforts as lack of fairness, or who might feel slighted or overlooked in favor of underrepresented groups. To address this, work with leaders to create hiring, promotion, and development processes that aren't biased or prejudiced. Coach them on how to evaluate individuals based on their skills, qualifications, and potential, rather than personal characteristics or connections. Your aim is to work with leaders to ensure that all employees understand how D&I initiatives benefit the entire organization and that everyone has equal opportunities for growth and advancement.

And this isn't only about policies and procedures. It's about culture. As a facilitator of professional growth, you must help the organization build an inclusive culture in which everyone feels valued and supported. Help them implement regular training and awareness programs, set up employee resource groups, and create initiatives that celebrate diversity. An inclusive culture is one in which individuals are motivated to bring their whole self to work and feel like they belong to a tribe, whose common purpose they embrace.

Another thing you will need to support as a coach is diverse representation. Work with the organization to ensure that diversity is reflected at all levels, especially in leadership positions. Push the organization to hire from groups that are often underrepresented. Help them see the benefits that come from employing different groups of people from different backgrounds and settings. Help them realize that when diverse people are represented, different voices get heard and, ultimately, biases and stereotypes are broken down.

Finally, as a performance coach, you have to keep the organization focused on continuous improvement. D&I practices and policies need to be regularly assessed and refined. A rigorous process must be developed for checking in on how the initiatives are tracking, eliciting feedback from employees, analyzing data on diversity, and benchmarking against best practices in the respective industry. Your role is to keep organizations committed to adapting and improving their approach over time.

The Role of Performance Coaching in Promoting Diversity and Inclusion

Performance coaching has a crucial role to play in cultivating diversity and inclusion. Helping people and organizations become more inclusive, reduce bias, and get the best out of diverse talent by lifting their capabilities will, in turn, help all employees feel valued, secure, and more confident to perform at their best.

But how do we do it? We never stop raising awareness. We ask the uncomfortable questions, getting people to think about D&I. We challenge our employees (for better or for worse) to reflect on how their own biases and assumptions might be impacting their decision-making, even their behavior. It isn't always pretty, but it's always necessary.

However, our job doesn't end with the individual employee—we also work directly with leaders to enable them with the tools to lead and manage all of a diverse team's members. It's our job to guide leaders through understanding that leading a diverse team comes with its own unique set of challenges and opportunities. We provide them with strategies for fostering a sense of belonging and empowerment among all team members. It's important to equip them with inclusive leadership skills to ensure that D&I is a top priority at the highest levels of the organization.

Now, let's talk about the impact we can have on diverse talent. As performance coaches, we can support those within underrepresented groups by giving the additional developmental experience they might need to break into a senior role, as well as by increasing access to these opportunities to help level the playing field.

And it doesn't stop there. We also play a critical role in promoting open and honest communication around D&I issues. We create a space where people can share their experiences and perspectives. We make sure that feedback can be given and received. We help build trust, understanding, and empathy among team members, by facilitating these conversations.

We also have to accept the hard truth that we're indeed all biased—whether we like it or not. And yes, let's be real for a minute, we all are. But, in our coaching role, we have the tools and techniques to help individuals recognize and address those biases. Through self-reflection and role-playing exercises, we can provide techniques for overcoming biases and driving more equitable behaviors and decisions across the organization. It's important to approach these conversations with empathy and understanding, while still holding individuals accountable for their actions and decisions.

Ultimately, it's our responsibility and role as performance coaches to help plant, nurture, and expand a diverse and inclusive culture that embraces all people in their fullest expression. We work with leaders and teams on how to cultivate a cultural climate that makes all employees feel like they belong and have full access to opportunities, where they're encouraged and celebrated for being themselves and for bringing their whole selves to work. We help organizations celebrate differences, encourage authenticity, and provide equal opportunities for success. By building a strong foundation of inclusion, we unlock the full potential of their diverse workforce. And when a diverse workforce is firing on all cylinders? That's when innovation, creativity, and business success reach new heights.

Strategies for Promoting Diversity and Inclusion Through Coaching

Lastly, let's explore some common tactics that can really move the needle on diversity and inclusion in the organizations we work with.

First things first, we need to systematically integrate D&I into our coaching programs. This isn't just a nice addition. It's a must-have. If you make D&I central to your performance coaching—with milestones and KPIs that you track—you are signaling that it's a genuine priority for you. And your people will pick up on it.

But we don't just pay lip service to D&I. As coaches, we can and must do much more to empower ourselves and our employees with tools that create real change. Unconscious-bias training, for example, is one such tool. We must help our employees recognize and address the biases that can influence their decision-making or how they interact with one another. It's not always comfortable. Still, it must be done.

Another key strategy is developing inclusive leadership competencies. This is where we can really help our employees shine. Getting leaders to focus on cultural intelligence, empathy, and inclusive decision-making manages to do two things at once. First, it paints an image of what leaders should be doing to create a culture where each and every one of their employees feels seen and heard. And two, it encourages leaders to lead by example. And when they do, it trickles down to the rest of the organization.

Now, let's turn our attention to employee resource groups. ERGs can provide such a powerful source of community and support for diverse employees, even if they often need some extra TLC to really thrive. And that's where we come in. By using performance coaching to support the development and success of ERGs, we can help create a sense of belonging and empowerment for diverse talent.

We must also advocate for mentorship and sponsorship programs that pair talent from underrepresented groups with sponsors who can teach them and provide them with career-advancement opportunities. That kind of relationship can be life-changing for these employees, and as coaches, we can help to make those connections.

Of course, none of this works without accountability. That's why D&I goals are so important—and why they must be set and tracked systematically. By helping our employees get clear about specific, measurable goals, then holding people to them using coaching and performance-management systems, we can help them actually improve.

But perhaps more importantly, we need to create safe spaces that encourage candid dialogue about D&I. Easier said than done, I agree. Especially if and when emotions are on high. Still, remembering that we have the training and experience to facilitate these dialogues respectfully and empathetically, we can invite our employees to share their experiences and perspectives—and bridges will be built, crossings created, over these treacherous terrains of bias and discrimination.

And finally, all of this leads to the underestimated benefit of powerful group dynamics: the ways that these differences between people can stimulate innovation and creativity. As performance coaches, we can help teams harness the diversity of their members' contributions, leading to better problem-solving and decision-making. Everybody wins.

Workplaces are evolving, and rather rapidly, so we must also evolve our coaching strategies. The following chapter will address the unique challenges and opportunities of coaching in remote and hybrid work environments.

CHAPTER IX

Adapting Coaching Strategies for Remote and Hybrid Work Environments

Opening Case: Adapting to Remote Work

Consider a global tech company facing challenges maintaining employee engagement and performance as they transition to a fully remote workforce. The company redesigns their approach to internal coaching, taking into account what remote work environments require to succeed. To support these changes, they develop new ways of using their virtual-meeting resources, such as Zoom and Microsoft Teams, to facilitate remote coaching sessions. Coaches schedule regular virtual check-ins with employees to provide continuous support and maintain engagement.

Coaching schedules are adapted to accommodate different time zones and employees' work-life balance. The company also organizes virtual team-building activities to strengthen team cohesion and collaboration despite physical distance. Coaches provide resources and training on remote-work best practices, helping employees navigate challenges effectively.

As a result, high levels of employee engagement are maintained. Employees adapt well to remote work, maintaining or even improving their performance levels. The flexible coaching schedules accommodate employees' diverse needs, leading to higher satisfaction and work-life balance. Virtual team-building activities foster stronger team dynamics, ensuring effective collaboration and communication.

The Importance of Adapting to Remote and Hybrid Work

Have you looked around recently? It seems like, over the past few years, there's been a seismic shift in what work looks like. Suddenly, most of our employees are on hybrid schedules or working from kitchen tables. We've all been thrown into a new, remote-hybrid world. As coaches, we can't just sit back and watch this unfold—we need to adapt our strategies to support our employees in these new remote and hybrid environments. Technology plays a crucial role in enabling effective remote coaching. We'll dive deep into specific tools and platforms in chapter XIII, but throughout this chapter we'll touch on how technology supports various remote coaching strategies.

Now, I know some of you might be thinking, "But remote work is great! People have more flexibility, better work-life balance, and can even work in their pajamas!" Fair enough. I've also witnessed just how transformational flexible work-from-anywhere policies can be for organizations. With the ability to hire talent globally, offer better productivity and a more stable cost structure, and foster employee well-being, it's a win-win scenario.

But let's be honest—these emergent ways of working also come with their fair share of challenges. If it's our role to coach people through these choppy waters, we have to be alert to the pitfalls that cause even experienced remote workers to bump their heads on their desks. Adapting to new work patterns, facing communication barriers, coping with isolation, dealing with different working hours, separating "work" and "life," being monitored on performance, maintaining healthy team dynamics—these are just a few of the unfortunate by-products of not going into an office.

How can we address these challenges? First, it's necessary to get creative with our coaching strategies. We need to get comfortable working virtually—leveraging as much "face-to-face" contact as we can through video calls, instant messaging, and virtual meeting rooms, always largely in real time. However, it's necessary to supplement this with something more. We have to focus on making sure people stay connected with each other—finding opportunities for our employees to schedule regular check-ins with their teammates, not just to talk shop, but to genuinely connect as human beings.

Isolation and loneliness? That's where we come in as coaches to help our employees build and maintain their professional networks. Suggest virtual coffee chats, a learning community, or a good old-fashioned phone call with another colleague. Help them understand that just because they're working remotely doesn't mean they should feel isolated.

And then there are the issues around the work-life boundary. In my own practice, I have witnessed too many burned-out work-from-home employees who feel that, because they are at home, they are always at work. As coaches we need to help them establish some anchor points and routine that draws the line between work and rest. Encourage them to keep a dedicated workspace, work regular hours, and take breaks between work activities. And most importantly, remind them that it's okay to unplug and prioritize their well-being.

If some managers are now finding it difficult to monitor performance remotely, well, that's because they lack trust—and that's something that our coaching can address. We can help supervisors identify the temptation to micromanage, helping them focus on setting clear objectives, providing regular feedback—positive and constructive—and making sure outputs, rather than face time, are measured.

Lastly, let's discuss team dynamics. If members of a dispersed team are overly individualistic, they'll never really become a team at all. The good news is that a group of people who work remotely can be just as cohesive and collaborative as a team of coworkers literally working together at the same location. Improving communication channels, agreeing on common goals, and giving members opportunities to bond and blow off steam are just as doable online as offline. Virtual team-building activities, anyone?

The Role of Performance Coaching in Remote and Hybrid Work

Let's map out ways we can be the support we know our employees need, as we all navigate uncharted waters in a remote-hybrid world.

First, we need to talk about communication. Any working relationship is dependent upon communication, but communication can be difficult when everybody is working remotely. As coaches, we help our employees find ways to communicate effectively with their stakeholders. One concrete piece of advice is to suggest that they overcommunicate, especially if they are worried about being too intrusive. When using videoconferencing applications, where possible, encourage them to carve out time for informal chats. We also have to model good communication with our employees. I recently worked with a new client in Japan who struggled with how to communicate when working remotely, so from the start

I included a short informal check-in at the beginning of each call about how they were doing.

But it goes way beyond this. Working remotely—at times, for many months on end—can be lonely and stressful. Managing resilience and reinforcing the importance of employee well-being, even if we can't offer that face-to-face contact, must become a real priority. Check that people are taking regular breaks, setting boundaries, and looking after themselves. Share with them the strategies you are using to stay grounded and manage stress. Most of all, share with them that they don't have to do it on their own. You have their back.

Now, on to productivity. There are probably days when working remotely leaves you feeling like nothing is getting done. By maintaining a consistent coaching approach and helping employees develop their own strategies, you can help them stay focused. That means managing their expectations, working with them to set clear, measurable goals, and breaking bigger assignments into smaller tasks. Celebrate each goal they reach. When they clear benchmarks more rapidly, that can give them the momentum to keep going toward their goal. And don't forget the value of accountability. Hold your employees accountable for the work they're performing. Ask them if they're keeping up with the assignments and check in to see if they're hitting their targets.

But true productivity is about always feeling part of a group—having a sense of belonging, engaging with the work, the group, and the goals, no matter how scattered. As coaches, we can maintain a sense of inclusion and belonging, even at a distance. Encourage employees to check in with teammates or fellow colleagues. Suggest virtual team-building activities. Encourage that specific employee to speak up in a meeting. And if you notice that employee succumbing to isolation, feel free to reach out, offer an ear or resources.

Time management is another big challenge in the world of remote work. How easy it is to let your life be taken over by work, when your office is just a few steps from your bedroom. As coaches, we help remote employees not only manage their time, but their energy. Make sure they stick to their schedule and develop a to-do list. Encourage them to set start and finish times for their day (and stick to them). And, above all, lead from the front: Share your own tips on how to get and stay productive and balanced.

Finally, let's not forget the leaders. Running a remote team is a totally different ball game, and it's our job to help them level up their approach. We work with leaders to develop what they need to lead their teams from afar, creating clear channels of communication, providing regular feedback and recognizing success, and fostering a culture of trust and autonomy. And, most of all, remind them that leadership isn't about control—it's about empowerment.

Strategies for Effective Coaching in Remote and Hybrid Work Environments

So, let's consider some strategies that can help to make your performance coaching more effective in this brave new world of remote and hybrid work. A lot has happened in the workplace in the past couple of years—a bit of a tumultuous ride. But by focusing on a few simple principles, we can still help set our people up for success, wherever they're working from.

First and foremost: embrace technology. Sure, you might like traditional, face-to-face performance coaching; however, virtual coaching can be (arguably, nearly) just as good as in-person coaching. Given equal access to the right technology, videoconferencing, instant messaging, and other collaborative software, we can be just as valuable in the virtual space. And you don't even need to be "techie"! Just start slow, and within a short time you'll be virtually coaching your socks off! Plenty of tools and platforms exist to enhance your virtual coaching sessions:

- Videoconferencing platforms: Zoom, Microsoft Teams, and Google Meet[15] offer high-quality video and audio, screen-sharing capabilities, and virtual whiteboards for collaborative work.
- Project-management tools: Trello[16], Asana[17], or Monday[18] can help coaches and employees track progress on goals and action items between sessions.
- Digital note-taking and sharing: Tools like Evernote[19] or OneNote[20] allow coaches to take notes during sessions and share them securely with employees.
- Collaboration tools: Miro[21] or Mural[22] provide useful virtual canvases for brainstorming, mind-mapping, and visual collaboration during coaching sessions.
- Scheduling software: Calendly[23] or Doodle[24], and even

---

[15] Google. Available at: https://meet.google.com/
[16] Atlassian. Available at: https://trello.com
[17] Asana, Inc. Available at: https://asana.com
[18] Monday.com. Available at: https://monday.com
[19] Evernote. Available at: https://evernote.com
[20] Microsoft. Available at: https://onenote.com
[21] Miro. Available at: https://miro.com/
[22] Mural. Available at: https://mural.co
[23] Calendly. Available at: https://calendly.com
[24] Doodle. Available at: https://doodle.com

Outlook calendar[25], can streamline the process of booking coaching sessions across different time zones.

» Learning-management systems: Platforms like Coursera[26] or Udemy[27], and other open-source solutions like the excellent Chamilo LMS[28] (one of my favorites) and Moodle LMS[29], can be used to assign and track supplementary learning materials between coaching sessions.

» Feedback and assessment tools: 360-degree-feedback platforms or personality assessments can be integrated into coaching programs to provide data-driven insights.

These virtual-coaching practices can help maintain a strong coaching culture, as we'll explore further in chapter XII, even in distributed work environments.

But technology is just the vehicle. It's what you do with it that counts, and that's what those regular one-to-one check-ins and feedback do. Just because we can't be physically face-to-face does not mean we need to taper back on the communication. If anything, it should push us to do more of it! Set those regular check-in meetings, leverage them to celebrate wins, problem-solve issues, and keep those goals on track. And don't forget the power of feedback—it's like a GPS for success!

And I imagine you're thinking: *But every employee is different! How can we remotely coach with a one-size-fits-all approach?* Right again! Because, as a coach, ultimately, we have to be chameleons too. If every employee is different, then we also have to be able to flex our style and adjust to those

---

[25] Microsoft. Available at: https://outlook.live.com/calendar
[26] Coursera. Available at: https://www.coursera.org
[27] Udemy. Available at: https://www.udemy.com
[28] Chamilo. Available at: https://chamilo.org
[29] Moodle HQ. Available at: https://moodle.org

differences. What might work for one employee might not work for another, and that's fine! Our job is simply to be able to notice those differences and adapt to them.

Now, let's talk results. It's easy to get caught in the weeds of a remote work environment, but let's go back to the why of remote work—to win. In order for remote work to maximize success for all parties, your employees need goals that are clear and measurable, and then you need to make sure they're focused on the outcome. Trust me, when they start seeing those results roll in, it will feel like a shot of motivation straight to the veins! And it will help build that all-important trust and autonomy—the secret ingredients of successful remote work.

But results aren't everything. We also need to help our employees navigate the muddy field of work-life balance. When your couch is also your workplace, it's too easy for the lines to blur. As coaches, we are the voice of sanity, encouraging our clients to set firm boundaries, take care of themselves, and avoid burnout, while sharing our own strategies, being an ear for venting, and, most importantly, being a role model for healthy work-life maintenance.

And let's not forget about the power of the team. The fact that everybody works remotely doesn't mean that teamwork is over either. On the contrary, it's more important than ever! Use your coaching superpowers to help teams build strong virtual connections, collaborate effectively, and maintain that critical sense of cohesion. Encourage virtual team building, regular check-ins, and a culture of open communication. Because when the team rows in the same direction, there's nothing they can't achieve!

These strategies are certainly useful for fully remote teams, but the unique challenges of hybrid work environments require specifically tailored coaching strategies. When coaching leaders, we might encourage them to make sure that remote and in-office employees receive the same level of development, visibility, and career advancement. We should also help leaders and employees recognize and mitigate potential biases that may arise from having some team members in the office while others work remotely. Strategies should be developed to maintain effective communication between in-office and remote team members, such as establishing communication norms and leveraging both synchronous and asynchronous tools. And we can work with employees to develop strategies for maximizing productivity and work-life balance in a hybrid environment, including how to structure in-office days for collaboration and remote days for focused work.

Furthermore, performance coaching can assist leaders to refine the competencies required for hybrid-team management (for instance, fostering trust, establishing clear team expectations, and providing consistent feedback across different work arrangements); we can also cocreate team-building and company activities that are accessible to employees working part- or full-time from home and those working on-site.

And finally, don't underestimate the value of training. Remote and hybrid work is new for many and comes with its own set of challenges. As coaches, it's our responsibility to give our employees the tools they need to succeed. From effective communication to time management to tech mastery, there's always room for growth. So don't be afraid to do it: Offer training sessions, share your best practices, and always be known as a consistent source of learning.

With a comprehensive understanding of various coaching contexts, it becomes important to assess the effectiveness of our efforts. The next chapter will guide you through measuring the success of your coaching programs and implementing continuous-improvement strategies.

CHAPTER X

Measuring Success and Continuously Improving Coaching Programs

Opening Case: Evaluating Coaching Program Success

Consider an airline company from the Middle East implementing a coaching program aimed at enhancing the skills of its senior managers. A comprehensive evaluation framework is designed to assess the impact of the program. Specific key performance metrics are listed around productivity, leadership effectiveness, and organizational engagement. Assessments are taken at the outset to determine the initial level of performance of each participant.

Coaches track progress by checking in regularly with participants and providing performance reviews, while using predefined metrics to track improvements. Feedback is solicited from participants on their coaching experience via surveys and one-on-one interviews. The firm's HR department analyzes this data, thus measuring the program's effectiveness and its relative success and areas for improvement. Post coaching, leadership skills improve across the board for selected participants (e.g., ability to manage teams and make upper-management decisions), and employee-engagement scores rise, indicating higher employee job satisfaction and motivation. Overall, productivity improves as managers apply their newly acquired skills from the coaching program. Participants provide positive feedback, highlighting the program's value in their professional development. The firm uses the evaluation results to refine the coaching program, ensuring it remains effective and aligned with organizational goals.

The Importance of Measuring Success in Coaching Programs

Let's talk about the single most important element—I would argue the one that makes or breaks any coaching program of quality—measurement. While measurement may seem tedious, it's an important aspect of effective coaching programs. It's ultimately the key to making sure our coaching programs are actually making a difference.

Suppose you've put in hours and hours to help employees get a better handle on the vicissitudes of work and life, as well as pursue goals instead of simply coping. How will you know that it's your coaching that's making the difference? The answer is measurement.

Well, "measurement" might sound a little dry, but please don't recoil just yet—I'm not proposing that you add a column of numbers to yet another company spreadsheet. It's actually about (yes, again) ensuring that you are doing work that adds value for your employees and their organization.

Think about it this way—when we measure the success of our coaching programs, we're holding ourselves accountable. We're saying, "Hey, we're not just here to chat and offer a few words of wisdom. We're here to make a tangible difference." And when we can show that our coaching is achieving the desired outcomes and meeting expectations, it's like a big stamp of approval on our work.

In fact, accountability is often only the beginning. When we measure what's happening, we also gain the information necessary to make decisions—whether or not to pivot our coaching—in real time: a GPS for our coaching programs. When we measure regularly, we not only gain insight on what we're achieving, we also determine where we need to course correct so we ensure we're headed in the right direction.

And let's not forget about the power of continuous improvement. By measuring what matters, you're rewarding yourself for doing the right thing. And you're also recognizing areas where you can grow and do more. You're creating a renewable feedback cycle that keeps raising the stakes and the level of value you provide your employees with.

But perhaps above all else, measurement enables our coaching programs to remain focused on our largest-scale stakeholders, keeping our results and recommendations aligned with the business's larger strategic intent. Great companies thrive when their people are performing well. Our job is to help the business demonstrate how performance coaching is moving their key performance indicators. And when we do it right, it sounds like music to the ears of the decision-makers who hold the purse strings.

And speaking of purse strings, let's not forget the importance of justifying the organization's investment in coaching. Discussing financial aspects can be uncomfortable, but it's necessary, as performance coaching programs require resources—time, energy, and, yes, cold hard cash. Demonstrating the success of what we do, proving the competence of individual success efforts—and of the larger program—and showing it at a very visceral level is a powerful way to justify that investing in coaching is worth every cent to the organization. It's similar to having a secret weapon in your back pocket when it comes time to secure ongoing support and resources.

Key Metrics for Measuring Coaching Success

So, how do we measure the success of our coaching programs? While metrics and KPIs may seem daunting, they're essential for assessing coaching effectiveness. When it comes to designing and delivering coaching programs to achieve real transformation, I promise you these numbers are not to be feared, because they are the first step to understanding what's working and what's not.

Picture it: You just completed a great coaching session with an employee—she is inspired and motivated, and she feels ready to take over the world. You have a really great feeling about it. But how will you know if that feeling translates into real, tangible results? Metrics can help.

First up, let's talk about goal achievement. This is the bread and butter of coaching success, because this is what we work on—helping clients set big goals, then check them off like. Slam-dunk that big presentation that made you anxious? Land that promotion you've been striving for? Those are the kinds of wins that get coaches hot and bothered, and they're how we know our coaching is spot-on.

However, it's not just the big hoo-ha transformation goals that we track. Sometimes it's the subtle behavioral shifts that will ultimately make the biggest difference. Maybe our employee is a manager who's been struggling to communicate with their team. Through coaching, we help them develop those killer communication skills, and suddenly, their team is working like a well-oiled machine. That's the kind of behavioral change that might not show up on a spreadsheet. Still, it's a huge win in our book, because metrics are also about the human dimension.

Is human engagement increasing? Are employees more fulfilled in their work? Are they more likely to stay with the company for the long haul? The kinds of questions we need are not necessarily those that are currently asked. But employment-engagement surveys and feedback tools do provide the answers.

Of course, we can't forget about the numbers. Measures of performance—productivity, quality of work, customer satisfaction, or whatever the organization's customary metrics are—that are fair game for measuring coaching success. If we can help our employees boost those numbers, it's like hitting the coaching jackpot.

And beyond that, there's return on investment. Yes, there it is: money. Financial discussions are rarely easy, yet they're essential for evaluating coaching investments. Sure, nobody wants to think of fellow human beings as "assets," liable to be "written off" if they're not working out. But the fact is, performance coaching is an investment—and like any investment, we need to be able to say that it's being made good. By crunching the numbers and comparing the financial benefits to the costs, we can prove that performance coaching is more than just a warm and fuzzy feeling—it's a smart business decision.

Best Practices for Measuring Coaching Success

So, let's consider some best practices for how a coaching program might be measured for success.

Begin with goal setting. We must have a preliminary conversation with our employee about what it is they want to get out of the coaching. And not necessarily that cringeworthy, new-agey goal "to be a better leader." These goals need to be SMART, so we know exactly what they look like and when we have achieved them.

But it's essential to be concerned with measuring success

beyond just analyzing numbers. Yes, we can and should measure success with quantitative data such as sales figures, productivity rates, or other comparable data points. However, it's also necessary to hear the qualitative feedback so that we can understand how the coaching process is making the employee's daily reality richer. It's like a puzzle: Quantitative data wraps around, giving us the corners, but to make the picture look real, and bring the experience to life, you must hear the qualitative feedback.

But how do we know if performance coaching is really making a difference? Well, one way is to establish a baseline measurement. Before we even start coaching, we take a snapshot of where our employees are at. What are their current performance levels? What are their biggest challenges and pain points? This gives us a starting point to measure progress against.

However, we don't just take this measurement once and walk away—we have to check our pulse throughout the coaching engagement. It's important to ask for data and feedback from our team members and stakeholders on a regular basis. Frequent measurement helps us ensure we're steering in the right direction and enables us to switch up the path if needed.

And speaking of stakeholders, you need to bring them into the measurement process, and the more the better, as long as they are relevant to the process. Coaching doesn't happen in a vacuum, but in an ecosystem, and you need that ecosystem to determine if and how much coaching moved the needle.

Of course, it can seem overwhelming to collect all this data. But there are so many tools at your disposal to track and measure, to access that information at your fingertips. These tools are akin to having a virtual assistant managing all the moving pieces, and many solutions exist to facilitate this work:

» Coaching-management platforms: Tools like Coaching. com[30] or Quenza[31] offer features for goal setting, progress tracking, and assessment.

» Survey tools: SurveyMonkey[32], Qualtrics[33], Google Forms[34], or my favorite open-source solution, LimeSurvey[35], can be used for collecting feedback from employees and stakeholders.

» Performance-management software: Platforms like 15Five[36], Lattice[37], or BambooHR[38] can track key performance indicators over time.

» Learning-management systems: Cornerstone OnDemand[39] or SAP SuccessFactors[40] can help track coaching-related learning and development activities.

» Data-visualization tools: Tableau[41] or Power BI[42] can help create compelling visual representations of coaching impact.

---

[30] Coaching.com. Available at https://www.coaching.com
[31] Quenza. Available at https://www.quenza.com
[32] SurveyMonkey. Available at https://www.surveymonkey.com
[33] Qualtrics. Available at https://www.qualtrics.com
[34] Google Forms. Available at https://forms.google.com
[35] LimeSurvey. Available at https://www.limesurvey.org
[36] 15Five. Available at https://www.15five.com
[37] Lattice. Available at https://www.lattice.com
[38] BambooHR. Available at https://www.bamboohr.com
[39] Cornerstone OnDemand. Available at https://www.cornerstoneondemand.com
[40] SAP SuccessFactors. Available at https://www.sap.com/products/hcm/solutions.html
[41] Tableau. Available at https://www.tableau.com
[42] Power BI. Available at https://powerbi.microsoft.com

▶ AI-powered analytics: Platforms like IBM Watson Talent[43] or Visier[44] can provide predictive insights on coaching effectiveness.

Still, collecting data is only a starting point. For datasets to be useful, we actually have to dive into the numbers—and the feedback—to tease out clues about trends and insights. We become detectives at a certain point, following the data breadcrumbs to facts about what's working, what's not, and where we can improve. Advanced analytics and data-visualization tools, which we'll explore in chapter XIII, can transform raw coaching data into actionable insights for program improvement.

And when we've cracked the case, we have to share what we've found with those who have a stake in the coaching program. This means not only reporting the results of coaching evaluations to our employees, their senior leadership teams, and other stakeholders, but also building trust from the organization by showing that performance coaching is working and delivering genuine value.

However, we should not forget the potential challenges or limitations in measuring coaching success. It can indeed be challenging to isolate the impact of coaching from other factors influencing performance. The full effects of coaching may not be immediately apparent either, making short-term measurement challenging. And, some coaching outcomes, like improved self-awareness, can also be difficult to measure objectively.

In addition, collecting detailed data on employee performance and development may raise privacy issues and lead to situations where employees or stakeholders are reluctant to participate in extensive evaluation processes.

Lastly, remember that focusing too heavily on quantitative

---

[43] IBM Watson Talent. Available at https://www.ibm.com/watson/talent
[44] Visier. Available at https://www.visier.com

measures may overlook important qualitative impacts, and that measuring success is itself a work in progress. It's not about reaching a destination, but about learning, growing, and getting better all the time. Every coaching engagement is an opportunity to refine our approach, try new strategies, and push ourselves to be better coaches.

Strategies for Continuous Improvement in Coaching Programs

The key to a highly effective coaching program is continuous improvement. It might not sound as exciting as "transformational breakthroughs" or "life-changing insights," yet it's the key to making sure our coaching stays fresh, relevant, and laser focused on delivering results.

But I'm already trying to do a million things as a coach. What's the deal, how can I possibly fit continuous improvement into it as well? I get where you're coming from. It does seem like yet another demanding initiative. The reality, though, is that continuous improvement is none of this. It doesn't have to be expensive. It usually isn't a big deal. It's simply about the little things that you do every day, consistently, to keep your craft sharp and your audience involved.

How then do we do this? We start by staying attuned to what our employee wants to achieve. Not just once at the onset of a coaching engagement, but regularly—checking in, reviewing, and revising the employee's goals as life and work change and evolve. These regular check-ins are essential since a coaching engagement is, again, in many ways like a GPS. We're always checking to be sure that we're driving in the right direction.

Still, we're not going to do it on the basis of pure intuition. It's essential to gather input from the people who matter most. And that's where feedback loops enter the picture. We need to design ways for our employees, their colleagues, and anyone else with a stake in the coaching to provide their thoughts, experiences, and insights from the process, good or bad. It's comparable to having our own board of directors, helping us see our coaching from every angle and identify areas where we can step up our game.

Clearly, not everything we're going to try is going to work, so continuous improvement must involve not just correcting what isn't working but also amplifying what is. So, along the way, it's necessary to build a culture of learning and development in our coaching practice and among the organizations with which we work. We have to be enablers, creating a growth mindset that encourages our employees and their teams to seek coaching, try new things, take on new challenges, and never stop learning. When we create that kind of environment, continuous improvement becomes a natural part of the way people work.

And let's not forget about ourselves in this equation. We must continue to keep learning as performance coaches. We must make it a point to connect with other great coaches, invest in our own training and development, stay up-to-date on the latest trends and best practices in coaching, and always look for ways to expand our toolbox. Be both the teacher and the student at the same time, continually learning and then applying this learning to your employees.

Okay, so now you're thinking: *But what if I make changes to my coaching program and they don't work?* Well, sometimes they don't. However, failure is also where some of your best learning opportunities come from. The important thing is to track the effect of the changes we make in and for the people we serve; to collect data and feedback and to use that information in a decision loop about what works, what needs to change, and what needs to go.

And when things go well? Then it's time to celebrate!

Recognizing and celebrating when our activities or ideas or products go well is an important part of continuous improvement. It keeps us motivated, energized, and ready for the next challenge. And when things do go wrong? (Because they do go wrong sometimes.) Then it's time to shake it off, learn from the experience, and use it as fuel for our next iteration.

Understanding how to measure success sets the stage for implementing robust coaching programs. In the following chapter, we'll discuss practical strategies for rolling out and sustaining effective coaching initiatives across your organization.

CHAPTER XI

Implementing and Sustaining Coaching Programs

Opening Case: Launching and Sustaining Coaching Programs

Consider again the German automaker, mentioned in chapter VI, deciding to pilot a coaching program to enhance employee development and improve overall performance. They follow a structured approach to ensure the program's success. The company clearly defines the objectives of the coaching program, focusing on improving customer service and employee retention. Internal and external coaches are selected based on their expertise in retail operations and employee development.

Individualized coaching plans are developed for each employee, complete with specific goals, action steps, and timelines. Communication about the program is provided to all employees through meetings, emails, and informational sessions that describe the benefits and expectations of the program. An initial workshop kicks off the coaching program, formally introducing the coaches and highlighting the coaching process, and after that, coaches hold regular check-ins with employees to follow up, give feedback, and adjust coaching plans where necessary. The company ensures sustainability of the coaching program by conducting ongoing training of the internal coaches and evaluating the program periodically. The results are that, according to employee reports, there are substantial increases in their skills and performance, especially in their customer service. The program also increases employee morale and reduces turnover. Better employee skills lead to increased interaction and satisfaction with customers, which, in turn, lead to higher customer-satisfaction scores. The program's structured approach and sustainability measures ensure its long-term success and continuous improvement. The coaching program fosters a culture of continuous learning and development within the organization.

Steps for Implementing a Coaching Program

Creating a coaching program requires a strategic and systematic approach to ensure sustainability and impact.

First, we are required to get very clear with the organization about what they're really trying to achieve with coaching. What's the endgame? Is it to improve employee performance? Or to build strong leaders? Or to cultivate a culture of continuous improvement, or something else? Being really clear on the purpose is like laying a foundation before a house is built. Without that first layer, nothing else works.

Still, you can't do this alone; the bigwigs need to buy in, too. Getting leadership buy-in helps establish initial resources, an infrastructure and dedicated support system for everything you want to do as a coach. Additionally, when the higher-ups are championing the program, it sends a message to everyone else that this is important work.

And when it comes to the coaches, be that your in-house

managers and HR professionals (if you are counting on what you already have) or outside experts, let's make sure they have the concepts, skills, and tools to do the job well. That means comprehensive training on everything from active listening and giving feedback to goal setting and confidentiality. We can't just throw them in the deep end and expect them to swim—we've got to give them the support they need to thrive.

However, training alone is not sufficient. We also need a coaching framework, a framework that defines the process, methodologies, and tools that we will be using to implement the coaching. In other words, our playbook. It has to do it all. It's got to cover assessments, action planning, feedback, and evaluation.

Of course, none of this matters unless you tell your employees about it and get their buy-in—people must understand what's in it for them and how they can contribute to broader organizational success. When people understand the purpose and benefits, they're more likely to engage and really run with it.

You might be thinking, *Let's just roll this out everywhere and see what happens!* But wait, it isn't that simple. Starting with pilot programs is the way to go. It gives us a chance to test the waters, gather feedback, and make tweaks before we go all in. And by selecting a small diverse group of participants, we can get insights from different perspectives.

However, it's important to be aware of the potential challenges and limitations in implementing sustainable coaching programs. First, some employees or managers may be skeptical of coaching or reluctant to participate fully. So, without strong backing from top management, coaching initiatives may struggle to gain traction. This is especially important because some benefits of performance coaching, like improved self-awareness or better decision-making, can be difficult to quantify.

Then, maintaining trust and privacy in coaching relationships can be complex in organizational settings. Meanwhile, ensuring that all coaches follow the same standards and methodologies can be challenging, particularly because coaching approaches may need to be adapted to fit different cultural contexts within global organizations.

Also, expanding successful pilot programs to the entire organization can present logistical challenges, as limited budget, time, or qualified coaches can hinder program implementation.

And our job's not over when the program is up and running. We must keep our eye on the ball to stay on track, monitoring progress and measuring impact along the way. This is where data is our friend. Keeping tabs on key metrics like performance improvements and employee engagement, we can see what's working and what needs a little TLC.

Finally, after refining the program based on initial results, we need to expand its implementation across the organization. But scaling doesn't mean setting and forgetting—we've got to make sure there's ongoing support and ample resources for both coaches and participants. This is a marathon, not a sprint, and sustainability is the name of the game.

Best Practices for Sustaining Coaching Programs

So, how do we ensure we continuously create value from our coaching programs? For those of you who have been coaching for a while, I suspect that your experience is similar to mine—building and sustaining these programs is not a one-and-done challenge. It's about weaving performance coaching into the fabric of the organization's culture and development strategy.

As such, the first step is to keep our own skills sharp. I know, I know, it's easy to get complacent when we're the ones doing the coaching. However, investing in our own ongoing training and development makes us better coaches. But just as importantly, it demonstrates to our employees that we are in this learning thing together. It's a great opportunity to model the very behavior we're encouraging in others!

In addition, coaching can't just be an isolated initiative. The real force-multiplying benefit arises only when it's embedded into HR processes. If coaching becomes part of performance reviews, talent-development plans, and succession strategies, it will be an inherent part of how the organization develops and manages its people.

Of course, you know all this is easier said than done if the culture doesn't encourage coaching. That's why we need to be advocates of a coaching culture—we should encourage employees to give, ask for, and receive feedback, set development goals, and view efforts for continuous learning and constant improvement as a lifestyle. And when we see that this coaching reaps the rewards of better engagement, higher retention, and bottom-line results, we should celebrate the victories so others know performance coaching works, and that it's worth it.

By now, some of you are already raising your eyebrows and asking yourself, *But coaching is all about personal connection! How can technology help that?* Well, I would like to tell you that, by leveraging the right tools—performance-management systems, feedback platforms, and virtual coaching—you can actually further enhance your coaching practice, as well as monitor and track performance management and feedback. Don't be afraid to engage with technology!

And how do we measure impact? Assessing the effectiveness of our coaching programs on an ongoing basis through quantitative and qualitative measures is key—not just for talking-points reporting, but to help us continue improving and applying the continuous-improvement principles from chapter X.

Supporting our coaches and participants is key to sustainability. This means giving them ongoing access to tools, training, and continued development. Allow them to learn from each other and create an environment where they can share ideas, best practices, and good stories. After all, we're all in this together.

Lastly, let's remind ourselves why we're doing this in the first place. We're not just coaching for coaching's sake; we're contributing to something bigger. We align the coaching programs we put in place to what the company wants to achieve, thereby giving meaning to our coaching work. We're essentially laying the groundwork for the coaching culture we'll examine in the next chapter.

Implementing a coaching program is only the beginning. What will truly transform your organization is your ability to foster a coaching culture. The next chapter will explore how to embed coaching principles into your organization's DNA.

CHAPTER XII

Sustaining a Culture of Coaching

Opening Case: Building a Coaching Culture

Consider a manufacturing company in Malaysia aiming to establish a coaching culture to improve employee performance and engagement. They need to integrate performance coaching into day-to-day management and leadership activities. There is buy-in from the top, the leadership team leading by example and engaging in coaching activities themselves. They develop training programs for managers and leaders to build their coaching capacity.

Coaching conversations are integrated into regular performance reviews, ensuring continuous development and feedback. Coaching workshops are organized regularly for managers to reinforce good practice and to provide them with further support and resources to build their coaching skills. The company implements reward and recognition systems to celebrate coaching successes and motivate employees. Employees are encouraged to provide regular and continuous feedback on coaching practices.

The introduction of the coaching culture has a number of measurable impacts. It leads to significant improvements in employee performance and productivity. As employees begin to feel truly valued and supported, they become more engaged and satisfied with their jobs. Managers and senior leaders develop better-calibrated coaching skills to support and develop their employees. Open dialogue and collaboration grow across the company. Crucially, coaching practices are embedded into the organization's culture, thereby assuring the sustainability of the coaching initiatives and the organization committing to continuous improvement.

The Importance of a Coaching Culture

Creating and sustaining a coaching culture is definitely close to my heart. *Coaching culture? That sounds like a bunch of corporate mumbo jumbo.* But hear me out—it's your ticket to long-term organizational success.

Imagine you're in an organization where everyone—and I mean everyone—is committed to continuous learning, development, and improvement. If you walk into the job to only nail the basics, clock in and clock out, and keep your head down, you will not be a valued member of the team. In a coaching culture, you acquire new skills, explore new opportunities, seek different roles, and strive to grow. That's because everyone else is doing it, too.

So why does it matter? Let me tell you a story. One of my clients was literally bleeding its best people. And no one inside could really explain why. Their employees seemed to be walking out the door at an alarming rate. There were no warning signs, no changes in the work environment—it was a mystery. But when I drilled down for more detail, the answer wasn't difficult to find. Employees felt they'd reached a glass ceiling, a job that led nowhere. The work itself wasn't the problem, their relationship with the company was.

That's where the unique dynamic of a coaching culture comes into play. In established coaching cultures, employees expect that they'll receive ongoing support and development. These cultures create teams who feel that their organizations are invested in them. They feel that they're part of a bigger project, one worth staying in for the long haul.

Yet a coaching culture isn't about retention only; it's about performance. Give employees the know-how, resources, and support to execute tasks and master their roles, and they will soar. Productivity will soar, quality will soar, and job satisfaction will soar. This approach can significantly enhance your organization's capabilities and performance.

And let's not forget about leadership development. In a coaching culture, leaders aren't just born, they're made. By providing emerging leaders with the guidance and support they need to grow and succeed, you create a succession plan littered with new leaders who have everything they need to break into the next step of your organization's growth. Think of it like planting a garden—with the right nurturing and care, those seeds of potential will blossom into something truly extraordinary.

But perhaps the most important reason for a coaching culture is the sense of alignment it creates. There is arguably no more potent way to secure this than through the creation of an ethos that is shared mutually by all team members. A coaching culture truly ensures that everyone is on the same page, working together toward a common purpose.

Best Practices for Sustaining a Coaching Culture

We want to ensure we sustain that coaching culture for the long haul. *Sustaining a coaching culture? That sounds like a lot of work!* And you're not wrong; however, the effort is worthwhile. When you make performance coaching an integral part of your organization's DNA, the payoff is nothing short of transformational.

So, where do you start? A critical factor in sustaining a coaching culture is leadership commitment. If the leadership team doesn't become passionate and committed to performance coaching, your journey will be an uphill one. Leaders modeling the way is absolutely essential—boasting the art of performance coaching; being coached by other internal or external coaches themselves; delivering on input and output metrics they commit to. Merely discussing coaching without demonstrating its value is not sufficient. People powerfully attune to exactly what is being done and what is not. When the leaders literally start walking the talk, it sends a compelling message that coaching is seriously valued.

However, it's not just about the leadership team. Performance coaching needs to be a core component of the organization itself. This means embedding it into your HR processes—right from performance management to talent development to succession planning. When performance coaching is a fundamental part of how you develop and support your employees, it becomes second nature.

But you can't close your eyes on the potential challenges you could face when trying to sustain a coaching culture. For starters, adapting coaching approaches to fit different cultural contexts within global organizations and providing ongoing training and support for coaching may strain organizational resources.

Plus, changes in leadership can definitely disrupt the continuity of a coaching culture, and ensuring all leaders and managers consistently apply coaching practices can be rather challenging, particularly because some benefits of a coaching culture, like improved trust or collaboration, can be hard to quantify. So, sustaining enthusiasm and commitment to performance coaching over time can also prove difficult.

Additionally, some employees or managers may be skeptical of performance coaching or reluctant to embrace a new cultural approach altogether, and balancing coaching activities with other work responsibilities may be difficult.

Naturally, you can't just expect everyone to become coaching experts overnight. Training and support are necessary ingredients here, so ongoing training on coaching competencies—coaching techniques, providing feedback, and measurement—will be important to building the capabilities. This also means celebrating coaching successes and rewarding good coaching behaviors to create a culture that encourages everyone learning to coach.

But let's be honest: Performance coaching can be a bit intimidating, especially if you have not been accustomed to giving or receiving feedback. This is another reason why building trust and creating an atmosphere for open dialogue can work so well. If employees feel comfortable seeking and offering feedback, performance coaching can truly take off. It's the kind of open space where vulnerability, honesty, and humility can meet equity, gratitude, and empathy.

And include technology. Leverage performance-management systems, feedback systems, options for virtual coaching, and more to help make coaching happen faster, more easily, and more effectively. It's like having a coaching tool kit at your fingertips to help you track progress, measure impact, and keep everyone on the same page.

Perhaps the most important thing to remember is that sustaining a coaching culture is an ongoing process. This is not a matter of set it and forget it, but of measuring, testing, and tweaking on a regular basis. As discussed in chapter X, with a mix of quantitative and qualitative metrics, you can evaluate the impact of your coaching programs after they're live and identify areas for improvement.

And, finally, lead by example. As a coach, you are demonstrating to your organization that lifelong learning and development is important, valuable, and fun. Attend coaching sessions (with your own coach), share what you learned in those sessions in your formal and informal communication, encourage your fellow coaching ranks to do the same, and find a way to evangelize that. Being a coach makes you better at what you do. By consistently modeling coaching behaviors, you can inspire widespread positive change throughout the organization.

As we've seen, coaching is a powerful tool for organizational development. In the next chapter, we'll explore how technology can enhance and scale your coaching efforts, making them more efficient and effective.

CHAPTER XIII

Integrating Technology Into Performance Coaching

Opening Case: Leveraging Technology in Coaching

Consider a US tech company leveraging technology to improve its coaching program. By integrating digital tools and platforms, they are able to provide more flexible and accessible coaching to employees. Coaches begin connecting with employees through videoconferencing platforms such as Zoom and Microsoft Teams, using other digital tools and platforms to deliver coaching, such as coaching software like CoachAccountable.com[45], which helps coaches track progress, set goals, and manage coaching plans.

Tools such as SurveyMonkey are used to gather employee feedback regarding their experience with the coaching. A learning-management system (LMS) is used to provide employees with access to training modules, resources, and coaching materials. Mobile apps are provided to employees to enable them to access coaching resources, reminders, and channels of communication via their mobile phones.

Coaching becomes more available to all employees regardless of their physical location. Access to coaches via virtual-meeting

---

[45] CoachAccountable. Available at http://www.coachaccountable.com

platforms and mobile apps means that employees are able to have remote access to coaching anytime, anywhere. Coaching software helps to increase tracking, follow-up, and accountability in terms of ensuring that targets set are met and that coaching initiatives are not derailed for any unstated reason. It tracks the flow and process of feedback. The convenience and flexibility offered by technology leads to higher employee engagement and participation in coaching activities.

The Role of Technology in Performance Coaching

As a performance coach, I've seen firsthand how technology has totally revolutionized the way we approach coaching. Gone are the days of expensive coaching programs that required coaches to be flown from halfway across the world, on a monthly or bimonthly basis, to deliver face-to-face sessions in stuffy offices. Long gone are the days where proponents of remote coaching like me (phone coaching, to be exact, in those days) were harshly criticized. Now, we've got a whole world of digital tools at our fingertips to make coaching more accessible, engaging, and, dare I say it, even fun!

What if you could coach your team from anywhere in the world? Imagine being able to get together with an employee, provide some feedback and support, and then simply log out and say, "See you later." No need to hunt down a conference room. No need to drive anywhere. No need to commit to a sometimes inflexible office schedule. With just one click, we can be truly responsive to any last-minute request and provide the timely support our employees need, when it matters, no matter where they are.

And that's not all—technology has also provided us with some pretty nifty ways to track performance and analyze data. I mean, who doesn't love a good graph or chart? Using digital platforms, it's now a breeze to collect feedback, track progress, and identify development gaps on the fly. It's like turbocharging our data-driven decision-making while keeping our team on track.

Let's talk about interactive learning. There is nothing like a boring corporate training session to put your employees to sleep. However, for companies, technology can make learning an interactive and even entertaining experience. Webinars, online courses, virtual simulations . . . be creative! If you can think it, chances are there is technology available to do it. Employees can learn whenever they want, how they want, and in a way that makes it easier for them to put that learning into action.

But perhaps the most valuable aspect of technology in performance coaching is the fact that we can plan for and engage with individual employees in ways that genuinely celebrate and respond to their uniqueness and needs. We can design programs truly befitting each learner.

⁜

Best Practices for Integrating Technology into Performance Coaching

How can we make the most of technology in our coaching sessions without losing that all-important human touch? As someone who has been using virtual reality as a tool to enhance my coaching as early as 2019, I've been there, trying to balance the cool new tech tools with the need to really connect with the employees. And it's partly a tightrope walk.

What helps me the most—or perhaps what I am still learning from—are some tricks I've collected over time.

First, it's important to pick the right tools, as using unsuitable technology can hinder rather than help the coaching process. We have to select platforms that help us achieve our goals, rather than disrupt them. Is it user-friendly? Does it integrate well with our other existing systems? These are some of the important questions we have to ask ourselves, as they directly relate to the potential challenges and limitations in integrating technology into our coaching programs.

Keep in mind that unequal access to technology can create disparities in coaching experiences. You should anticipate potential cultural differences, as technology preferences and acceptance may vary across cultures. Also, the constantly evolving technology landscape can be overwhelming, forcing coaches and employees to keep up with the rapid pace of innovation, on top of existing obligations.

Then, some coaches or employees may resist new technologies, as connectivity problems or software glitches can disrupt sessions. Furthermore, organizations also need to anticipate the sometimes-high initial investment and ongoing expenses for technology solutions, and balance that with the potential challenges they could face in trying to accurately evaluate the impact of technology on coaching outcomes.

One thing I've learned the hard way is that you can never underestimate the impact of good training! Remember that time you thought you could figure out a new platform on your own? Yeah, that time when things didn't go so well. Let's make sure we're giving our employees the knowledge they need to more effectively use these tools. And let's give them ongoing support too—we all need a helping hand sometimes, right?

But here's the kicker. Cool as any tech might be to use, it will never replace the human connection. Haven't we all gotten into coaching because of this in the first place? To connect with people, to help them grow. So, let's use technology to augment our interactions, not replace them. Personally, while today I conduct almost 90 percent of my interventions remotely, I always insist on the need to schedule good old face-to-face meetings.

One at the very beginning of the coaching relationship, to set the tone, build rapport, and evaluate chemistry. And then every three or four months to ensure a proper dynamic throughout the virtual coaching intervention. Think of technology as the sidekick to your coaching superhero, not the main character!

Now, I know this might sound a bit dull; however, in this age, we can't ignore the importance of data privacy and security. We're dealing with people's personal information here! It's essential to make sure we're using secure platforms and being up-front with our employees about how we're protecting their data. After all, technology or not, it's all about building trust, right?

We need to collect and store only essential information and obtain explicit consent for collection and usage. We have to use end-to-end encryptions for all communications and data storage and implement strict access controls and multifactor authentication, as well as set clear policies on data storage and deletion. And let's not forget about developing a plan for handling potential data breaches.

We also have to carefully evaluate and monitor any third-party service providers and use reputable, GDPR[46]-compliant coaching platforms and tools, in addition to conducting periodic security audits and vulnerability assessments. And, of course, we have to educate coaches and employees on data-protection best practices.

Finally—and this is the biggie—it's necessary to know whether this technology is working for us. Is our employee happy? Is it making our life easier, or is it adding to our headaches and taking our focus away from the task? Ask for some feedback when you can, and if something's not working, fix it.

---

[46] General Data Protection Regulation (GDPR). While it is a comprehensive data protection and privacy regulation in the European Union, its influence extends beyond the EU as many international organizations have adopted its principles as a global standard for data protection.

While technology offers powerful tools to enhance coaching practices, it's crucial to stay ahead of the curve. In our next chapter, we'll discuss emerging trends and directions for the future of performance coaching, helping you prepare for the evolving landscape of organizational development and employee performance.

CHAPTER XIV

Future Trends

Opening Case: Embracing AI in Coaching

Consider a Swiss-headquartered global corporation recognizing the potential of AI to enhance its coaching program. The company rolls out organization-wide, AI-powered coaching tools that provide employees with personalized recommendations, track progress, and include real-time feedback, hugely enhancing their coaching experience. Employee-performance data is analyzed using AI-powered assessment tools that identify specific coaching needs. These are then channeled into the creation of purpose-built coaching plans designed for specific needs and goals with the help of AI algorithms.

AI-driven platforms provide real-time feedback to employees, helping them make immediate adjustments and improvements. The AI tools continuously track employee progress, providing coaches with up-to-date information to guide their coaching sessions. AI-generated automated insights and recommendations for both employees and coaches enhance the overall effectiveness of the coaching program.

As a result, employees receive highly personalized coaching plans tailored to their specific needs and goals. Real-time feedback allows employees to make immediate improvements, accelerating their development. Continuous progress tracking ensures that coaching efforts are aligned with employee-development goals. AI-generated insights provide valuable data to refine coaching strategies and improve outcomes. Both employees and coaches report higher satisfaction levels with the coaching program, citing the effectiveness and efficiency of AI-powered tools.

Emerging Trends in Performance Coaching

I sympathize with today's younger coaches. They remember nothing about being novices during Excel's rise, and now we're already talking about artificial intelligence, telepresence, and even virtual reality in our coaching practices. Wild, right? Let me share some of the big trends I've been seeing (and have been experimenting with) in performance coaching.

First up, building on the technological foundations discussed in chapter XIII, let's explore upcoming innovations in AI-assisted coaching. Now, I know we're all thinking, *Is a robot going to take my job?* Not yet it's not! There's no Skynet[47] as of now, but AI is a fun teammate—a smart sidekick that provides helpful data that we might not otherwise notice. For example, just last month I was reviewing data for a client against some baselines using AI and it found something that I wouldn't have spotted on my own. Pretty neat, huh?

And that is just the beginning. Imagine an AI-powered chatbot that provides continuous coaching support to your employees, even when you're not available. This may include answering questions or providing reminders or coaching tips based on their specific collaborative goals and challenges. I have observed these being successfully implemented in organizations to maintain the

---

[47] The fictional artificial-intelligence system from the *Terminator* franchise.

momentum between sessions. And they are great.

Moreover, AI is revolutionizing how we approach personalized learning. By analyzing performance data, AI can generate tailored learning recommendations for each employee. For example, if the data shows a manager struggling with delegation, the AI might recommend specific resources, exercises, or even microlearning modules to address this skill gap. Essentially, it's similar to having a personal learning assistant for each of your employees.

What about you? Any high-tech ways to spice up your performance coaching recently? I started experimenting with virtual reality a few years ago (pre-pandemic) and it has really been a game changer for some of my interventions. Imagine being able to practice a critical strategic presentation or a difficult conversation in a virtual environment. No real-world consequences, yet all the learning benefits. It's like a safe playground for skill building!

VR (virtual reality) is great for leadership development. I was recently introduced to VR simulation products that take leaders and put them in the driver's seat of complex situations—like a crisis or a multicultural team that they need to lead and manage. The immersive nature of VR makes the learning stick in a way that traditional role-playing just can't match. Another exciting application of VR is in cultural-sensitivity training. With globalization, many of our employees are working in diverse, multicultural environments. VR can transport them to different cultural contexts, helping them understand and navigate cultural nuances more effectively. It's an incredibly powerful tool for developing global leadership skills.

And then there's the elephant in the room: remote work. How many of you are coaching people you've never met in the flesh? Now we're talking a completely different ball game for many. We sit in front of the screen and make our Zoom calls, we use our tech tools, and it's not the same, I am sure of that. But we can build just as strong employee-coach relationships virtually, if we're just prepared to change our method to fit the medium.

One of my favorite emerging trends is asynchronous coaching platforms, which allows for ongoing dialogue, goal setting and monitoring, and resource sharing between coaches and employees, without the two needing to be online at the same time. It's perfect for busy professionals or when working across different time zones.

Speaking of time zones, remote work has opened up incredible opportunities for global mentoring programs. I've been involved in initiatives where senior leaders from one part of the world coach up-and-coming talent in another, all facilitated through digital platforms. It's breaking down geographical barriers and creating rich, diverse learning experiences.

I have also been spending a lot of time lately thinking about well-being and resilience. In the past few years, chances are that you might have felt like you were riding the wildest roller coaster of your life. Many of us felt that way. We went through a global pandemic that significantly impacted how we lived and how we worked. Remember those days of roaming empty supermarkets for basic necessities and food? Remember the ever-changing restrictions imposed on our freedom of movement? Remember how technology was once the only lifeline we had to connect to the outside world? Thankfully, those days are behind us, though they're not that far back. Most economies have now also taken a turn for the worse. Tough times, right? Well, our employees are definitely feeling it too. I have noticed that more people seem to be struggling with stress and burnout. So, I've been spending more time integrating wellness strategies into my coaching interventions. For me, it's really all about helping our employees thrive in all aspects of their lives, be it personal or professional.

And speaking of thriving: As coaches, we can't ignore the

importance of diversity, equity, and inclusion in our performance coaching. I've done a lot of reading and self-reflection around this, thinking about how we can better support diverse employees or how we address our own biases. It's challenging work. Still, from what I've read and learned, companies that are going to thrive are those that create truly inclusive workplaces.

Lastly, let's talk data. I remember twenty years ago when "data-driven performance coaching" meant examining last quarter's sales figures or the results of an MBTI[48] test. Now we've got all sorts of analytics at our fingertips. And it's tempting to think it's all too much and not take the time to deal with it, to make sense of it. However, I've actually found that used well, data adds power to your coaching impact. The trick is to use it as a supplement, not a replacement.

As coaches, we can effectively use data analytics by:

- ▶▶ Creating performance dashboards to monitor real-time progress toward goals: We can track real-time data such as sales closed, leads generated, and customer-satisfaction scores. This gives us the opportunity to provide our employee with immediate feedback and also ensures the timely adjustments of our coaching strategy.
- ▶▶ Using predictive analytics to identify potential areas for improvement: We can use a project manager's past performance data to identify potential bottlenecks in upcoming projects. This ensures we're much more proactive in the way we design our coaching interventions.
- ▶▶ Leveraging sentiment analysis to gauge employee engagement: We can use insights and patterns from company emails and chat conversations to identify employees who might be struggling or disengaged. This

---

[48] Myers-Briggs Type Indicator (MBTI®) is a registered trademark of The Myers & Briggs Company. For more details, see The Myers-Briggs Company, "MBTI®". Available at https://www.themyersbriggs.com

ensures early intervention and support.

- » Applying A/B testing to different coaching methodologies: We can test two different goal-setting frameworks with different groups of employees and analyze the results to determine which approach leads to better outcomes.

- » Utilizing machine-learning algorithms to create action plans that are highly relevant and personalized: By analyzing data on an individual's learning style, past performance, and career goals, we could use AI to suggest tailored coaching interventions and resources that are most likely to resonate with each employee.

Challenges and Ethical Considerations

Yet, amid all these potential benefits, it's also crucial to consider the potential challenges and ethical implications these innovations could bring.

We will need to ensure that sensitive personal information that we gather during coaching sessions is securely stored and protected. This may involve implementing robust data-encryption methods, strict access controls, and regular security audits.

AI systems can and do inadvertently perpetuate or amplify existing biases. If historical performance data is a reflection of past discriminatory practices, for example, AI-powered coaching recommendations might mirror these biases. We therefore will have to check AI outputs for bias, and work, possibly, with data scientists to develop mitigation strategies. And while AI and data analytics can provide valuable insights, it's important not to become overreliant on technology. We should use it as a tool to enhance our practices, not to replace human judgment and empathy. This might require clear guidelines regarding when coaching insights should be guided by AI versus our personal experience and intuition.

Also, not all employees may have equal access to or comfort with technology-enhanced coaching tools. It's important to be mindful of this and ensure that our practices aren't inadvertently unfair toward certain groups. This might involve offering alternative coaching methods or providing additional support and training for technology use.

We should also be transparent about how we're using AI and data in our practice. This includes explaining to employees what data is being collected, how it's being analyzed, and how it informs coaching decisions. Doing so helps mitigate any potential concerns felt by employees around the use of technology in coaching. Furthermore, clear and informed consent to the collection of data and any AI applications needs to be sought. We need to prepare consent forms that clearly state what data is to be collected, how it will be used, and what the risks might be; employees should have the ability to opt out of certain kinds of data collection or AI-driven processes without it affecting their access to performance coaching.

Lastly, we have to ask: If AI starts making recommendations that lead to negative outcomes, who is responsible? We should work with our organizations and policymakers to establish clear guidelines for accountability in AI-assisted coaching.

Upon exploring the future landscape of performance coaching, it's clear that success comes down to having both adaptability and a diverse set of tools. In the final chapter, we'll explore a comprehensive tool kit of practical resources, templates, and techniques that you can immediately apply to enhance your coaching practice. This tool kit will help you put into action the principles and strategies we've discussed throughout the book, ensuring you're well equipped to face the evolving challenges of performance coaching.

CHAPTER XV

Supporting Performance Coaching with the Right Tool Kit

In this final chapter, I've compiled a small tool kit of practical resources designed to enhance the effectiveness of coaching interventions. Recognizing the critical importance of mastering foundational techniques, I've included detailed guidance on essential tools and templates. These range from goal-setting frameworks and task-prioritization methods to the nuanced differences between coaching action plans and individual-development plans (IDPs). We'll also delve into strategies for providing constructive feedback, encouraging self-reflection, and adopting a strength-based approach to coaching. Additionally, we'll cover techniques for developing active-listening skills, crafting open-ended questions, and helping team members set healthy boundaries. To ensure coaches can adapt to diverse learning styles, I've included information on various learning-style models and instrument-based assessments. Rounding out the tool kit is a behavioral-observation template for performance coaching. By offering in-depth explanations and practical applications of these tools, my aim is to equip coaches with the fundamental skills and resources necessary to maximize the efficiency and impact of their coaching interventions.

This chapter serves as a comprehensive reference, ensuring coaches can confidently apply these essential techniques in their practice.

SMART Goal Setting

Popularized by the article "There's a S.M.A.R.T. way to write management's goals and objectives" by George T. Doran in 1981, SMART, discussed in chapter II, is a mnemonic for defining goals (or objectives) that are specific, measurable, achievable, relevant, and time bound. Here's what each of those characteristics means:

Specific: How many times has somebody ever come to you and said they wanted to "get better at the job"? A lot, right? Okay, that's great. But how specific is that? And more importantly, what does that even mean? The whole point is that goals should tell us what we are aiming for, and how to get there. Goals help our employees focus—they'll now know just what it is they are trying to accomplish—and they should answer the five W questions: who, what, where, when, and why. An improved goal would sound more like, "I want to complete a leadership training program to enhance my management skills by the end of the year."

Measurable: The other thing about goals is that they have to tell us how we're going to measure progress. And if they don't, how will our employees ever know if they're getting closer to the finish line? This helps our employees stay on track, reach target dates, and create the sense of accomplishment that fuels the continued effort required to reach goals. So, rather than something like "increase customer satisfaction," why not think about increasing customer-satisfaction ratings by 10 percent in the next six months as a much more measurable goal?

Achievable: Goals need to be realistic and attainable. That

middle ground between challenging and impossible is so tricky. So, we have to consider the resources and constraints that might impact our employee's ability to achieve the goal. A good example? "I will secure five new clients for our consultancy firm within the next quarter by enhancing our marketing efforts and networking." Ambitious? For sure. But impossible? I don't think so.

Relevant: This is where many go wrong in goal setting—making promises that sound great but don't matter. Take me becoming a world-class juggler, for instance. Nice skill, but not really relevant to my coaching career. Goals should matter and have significance to the employee or organization setting them. They should align with other objectives and be worthwhile.

Time bound: every goal has to be time bound, with a start date and an end date. Without a deadline, a goal is just a wish. Want to bring a sense of urgency? Then definitely make it time bound. It's the difference between "I'll launch the new product one day" and "I'll launch the new product at the end of Q4."

When you combine all these elements, a SMART goal set might look like this:

- Specific: I want to complete a certification course in project management.

- Measurable: I will enroll in an online course, complete all modules, and pass the certification exam.

- Achievable: I will dedicate five hours per week to studying for the next three months.

- Relevant: This certification will improve my project-management skills and enhance my career opportunities.

- Time bound: I will complete the certification by the end of the current quarter.

There are many benefits to adopting SMART goals. They provide clear direction and focus. They offer tangible milestones to aim for, which can be motivating. Progress can be easily tracked, allowing for adjustments if necessary. And they ensure goals are realistic, reducing the risk of setting unattainable targets. Using this simple framework can greatly enhance your employees' ability to set and achieve objectives, whether in a personal or professional context.

Prioritizing Tasks

If you're managing and leading a team, one of the most effective ways that you can support your people to improve their productivity and go home with a full sense of achievement is to help them master the skill of prioritizing. Here are some strategies that you can employ to support your employees to better prioritize their own workload:

1. Understand your employees' current workload and how they are managing their tasks. This can be done through a one-on-one meeting where they outline their daily and weekly responsibilities. Encourage them to create a comprehensive list of all their tasks, including ongoing projects, deadlines, and routine duties.

2. Provide them with time-management techniques. You can introduce them to the Eisenhower Matrix (also known as the Urgent-Important Matrix) as a way to develop better prioritization skills. The matrix is useful as it categorizes tasks into four quadrants:

	IMPORTANT	NOT IMPORTANT
	Do First	**Delegate**
URGENT	**Tasks that are both urgent and important.** These tasks should be done immediately. *Examples: Crisis management, pressing deadlines.*	**Tasks that are urgent but not important.** These tasks should be delegated to others if possible. *Examples: Interruptions, some emails, routine tasks.*
	Schedule	**Eliminate**
NOT URGENT	**Tasks that are important but not urgent.** Schedule these tasks for later. *Examples: Planning, long-term projects, personal development.*	**Tasks that are neither urgent nor important.** Consider eliminating these tasks. *Examples: Time-wasters, trivial activities, some meetings.*

3. Encourage your employees to use time blocking, where they dedicate specific blocks of time to different tasks or types of work. This can help them ensure focused periods, for important tasks, without constant interruptions.

4. Recommend task-management tools like Trello (trello.com), Asana (asana.com), or Microsoft To-Do (to-do.office.com). These tools can help organize, track, and prioritize tasks visually. Encourage the use of digital or physical calendars and planners to schedule tasks and set reminders for deadlines.

5. Set those SMART goals.

6. At the end of each day, make sure your employees take the time to review what they have accomplished and

adjust their task list for the next day. And, at the end of each week, they should also review their progress toward weekly goals and their plan for the upcoming week. This helps in keeping track of long-term objectives and adjusting priorities as needed.

7. Go back to the Urgent-Important Matrix and help your employees identify tasks that can be delegated to others. This can free up their time for more critical tasks. Ensure that they feel comfortable delegating tasks and provide support in identifying suitable team members for delegation.

8. Stress the importance of taking regular breaks to avoid burnout. Short breaks can improve focus and productivity. Encourage them to set boundaries for work hours, especially if they are working remotely, to maintain a healthy work-life balance.

9. Schedule regular check-ins to discuss progress, address any challenges, and provide feedback. This can help employees stay on track and feel supported. And don't hesitate to offer mentorship or pair the employee with a more experienced colleague who can provide guidance on task prioritization and time management.

Example Scenario:

Background: A team member is overwhelmed with a high volume of tasks and struggling to prioritize effectively.

Steps:

1. Schedule a one-on-one meeting to discuss their current workload and challenges.

2. Ask the individual to create a comprehensive list of all their tasks.

3. Explain the Eisenhower Matrix and suggest using a task-management tool.

Example:

Let's say your team member has the following tasks:

- Complete project report due tomorrow (Urgent and Important)
- Plan team strategy meeting for next month (Important but Not Urgent)
- Respond to routine emails (Urgent but Not Important)
- Scroll through social media (Not Urgent and Not Important)
- Organize the task list accordingly:
- Complete project report would go in Do First.
- Plan team strategy meeting would go in Schedule.
- Respond to routine emails would go in Delegate.
- Scroll through social media would go in Eliminate.

1. Help the individual set daily and weekly priorities based on their goals.
2. Schedule regular check-ins to review their progress and adjust priorities as needed.
3. Identify tasks that can be delegated and support the team member in delegating them.
4. Provide continuous feedback and support, offering additional resources or training if necessary.

By implementing these strategies, you can help the team member develop better task-prioritization skills, leading to increased productivity and reduced stress.

Coaching Action Plan Versus Individual-Development Plans (IDP)

You might be wondering what exactly separates a coaching action plan from an IDP, and guess what, you're not alone! So here goes: A coaching action plan is similar to that weekend trip you're planning with a significant other, and an IDP is that cross-country trip you need some kind of Google-mapped plan for.

The Coaching Action Plan

The coaching action plan is the operational agenda within the coaching process that details the specific steps, activities, and time frames the employee will follow to meet the developmental goals they have identified during coaching sessions. It's very tactical and focuses on the "how" of reaching the goals identified within the broader coaching strategy. Significant attributes include:

- Direct focus on specific actions the individual needs to take.

- Although part of a broader goal, the action plan usually breaks down the process into smaller, more manageable actions that can be accomplished in the short-term.

- Regular feedback is necessary from the coach to assess the effectiveness of the actions and adjust as necessary.

- The individual is held accountable for taking the steps outlined in the action plan, with the coach providing support and accountability checks.

The best way to make sense of the coaching action plan is through the following sample:

Employee Name: Sarah Smith
Position: Marketing Specialist
Coach Name: Dr. Behar-Courtois
Date: June 1, 2024
Goal Setting:

Primary Goal:	To improve Sarah's presentation skills for client meetings.
Specific:	Sarah will complete a public-speaking course and deliver at least three presentations in client meetings over the next six months.
Measurable:	Success will be measured by completing the course and receiving positive feedback on the presentations from clients and peers.
Achievable:	Sarah has basic presentation skills and support from her team to enhance them further.
Relevant:	Improving presentation skills is crucial for Sarah's role in client engagement and aligns with the company's goal to improve client satisfaction.
Time bound:	The goal will be achieved by December 1, 2024.

Action Steps:

	Deadline	Actions	Resources Needed	Support Needed
(1) Enroll in a public-speaking course	June 15, 2024	Research online and in-person courses. Select and enroll in a suitable course.	Internet access, budget approval.	Guidance on course selection from manager.
(2) Complete the public-speaking course	August 31, 2024	Attend all sessions and participate actively. Complete assignments and practice exercises.	Course materials, dedicated time.	Regular check-ins with coach to monitor progress.
(3) Plan and prepare for presentations	September 15, 2024	Identify opportunities to present at client meetings. Develop and practice presentations.	Presentation tools, rehearsal space.	Feedback from coach and team members.
(4) Deliver presentations	November 30, 2024	Deliver at least three presentations in client meetings. Gather feedback from clients and peers.	Presentation materials, client-engagement tools.	Ongoing support from coach and feedback from attendees.
(5) Evaluate and reflect on presentations	December 15, 2024	Review feedback from presentations. Reflect on strengths and areas for improvement. Document lessons learned and plan for further development.	Feedback forms, reflective journal.	Facilitated review session with coach, feedback from peers.

Monitoring and Support:

Weekly Check-Ins:	Sarah will meet with Dr. Behar-Courtois every Friday to discuss progress, challenges, and adjustments needed.
Monthly Review:	A detailed review session will be conducted at the end of each month to assess progress and provide additional support if needed.
Feedback Mechanisms:	Sarah will seek feedback from clients and team members after each presentation.

Evaluation:

Criteria for Success	Measures of Achievement	Follow-Up Actions
Completion of the public-speaking course by August 31, 2024.	Course-completion certificate.	Continuous development: Identify additional areas for improvement based on feedback.
Delivery of at least three presentations by November 30, 2024.	Feedback forms from presentations.	Future projects: Plan for Sarah to take on more complex presentations and client engagements.
Positive feedback from clients and peers.	Reflective document on lessons learned.	Additional training: Recommend further training in advanced presentation techniques if needed.

The Individual-Development Plan (IDP)

The IDP is a longer-term development plan, focused around the individual's career-development goals and the activities required to achieve them. It's typically a broader-scope document than a coaching plan, as well as employee driven, with buy-in from their manager and potentially a coach. The key components to consider include:

- An IDP covers a broad range of developmental goals that are aligned not only with the employee's career aspirations but also with organizational needs.
- It contains a clear, detailed list of goals, with all the necessary steps, expected milestones, and timelines to achieve them.
- While it can include immediate goals, it often extends over a longer period, such as one to five years, in order to support long-term career development.
- It includes a variety of activities beyond coaching, such as training courses, reading, assignments, shadowing, or mentoring.
- And, although it may be supported by a manager or coach, or both, the primary responsibility for following through on an IDP lies with the individual.

Let's explore a sample individual-development plan:

Employee Name: Jane Doe
Position: Senior Analyst
Target Position: Team Manager
Date: June 2024
Review Dates: December 2024, June 2025

Career Objective
To develop the necessary leadership and management skills to transition from a senior analyst role to a team manager position within the next eighteen months.

Development Goals and Activities

Goal 1: Enhance Leadership Skills

Improve team leadership and conflict-resolution skills.

Activities	Success Metrics
- Attend the "Leadership Excellence" workshop by Q4 2024. - Read *The Five Dysfunctions of a Team* by Patrick Lencioni by Q1 2025. - Monthly mentoring sessions with current department manager.	- Receive at least 90% positive feedback in leadership skills from workshop assessment. - Implement conflict-resolution strategies in team projects, reducing team conflicts by 30% by Q2 2025.

Goal 2: Develop Financial-Management Understanding

Acquire advanced knowledge in budgeting and financial forecasting.

Activities	Success Metrics
- Enroll in the online course "Finance for Non-Financial Managers" by Q3 2024. - Shadow the finance department for one week in Q1 2025.	- Pass the course with a score of 85% or higher. - Apply learned concepts to develop next fiscal year's team budget.

Goal 3: Enhance Communication Skills

Improve public-speaking and presentation skills.

Activities	Success Metrics
○ Join and participate in Toastmasters by Q3 2024. ○ Deliver at least five presentations in team meetings by Q2 2025.	○ Receive constructive feedback from Toastmasters' mentors and apply it to improve speaking skills. ○ Achieve an average presentation feedback score of 4.5/5 from team members.

Goal 4: Project-Management Proficiency

Master advanced project-management techniques.

Activities	Success Metrics
○ Complete the "Advanced Project Management" certification by PMI by Q4 2024. ○ Lead two major projects from inception to delivery by Q3 2025.	○ Obtain certification with a passing grade. ○ Successfully deliver projects on time, meeting all specified goals and receiving positive feedback from stakeholders.

Support Required

- Approval for course and workshop enrollments.
- Support from HR for registration in Toastmasters.
- Scheduled time for shadowing and mentoring sessions.

Review and Adjustment

- Regular check-ins with supervisor every two months to discuss progress and any necessary adjustments to the plan.
- Formal reviews in December 2024 and June 2025 to assess progress against goals and realign activities if needed.

Employee's Commitment
I commit to actively engage in all outlined activities and seek regular feedback from my peers and superiors to ensure continuous improvement toward achieving my career objectives.
Employee:
Position:
Employee Signature:

Supervisor's Commitment
I commit to supporting Jane Doe in her developmental activities, providing necessary resources and offering constructive feedback to guide her progress toward her career goals.
Supervisor:
Position:
Supervisor Signature:

Providing Effective and Constructive Feedback

Providing effective and constructive feedback is a crucial skill for leaders, managers, and coaches. And yet, you would be surprised by the number of people I have crossed paths with who struggle, and even start profusely sweating, at the simple idea of providing feedback to an employee. So, here are some simple guidelines to help ensure your feedback is well received and leads to positive outcomes:

1. Focus on behavior, not the person: Address specific actions or behaviors rather than making personal comments. This keeps the feedback objective and negative emotions to a minimum.

2. Provide concrete examples to illustrate your points. This helps the recipient understand exactly what you're referring to.

3. The closer the feedback is given to the behavior, the more impactful it will be. Delayed feedback can lose relevance and effectiveness.

4. Start and end with positive feedback, giving constructive feedback in the middle. This "feedback sandwich" approach can make negative feedback more palatable.

5. Be genuine in your praise and criticism and avoid giving feedback that feels insincere or forced. People will pick up on you not being real.

6. Genuinely aim to help the recipient grow and improve by offering suggestions or solutions to address the issue rather than just pointing out problems.

7. Ask the recipient for their perspective on the situation as this can foster self-awareness and a collaborative approach to finding solutions.

8. Provide feedback in a private setting to avoid embarrassment and ensure a comfortable environment.

9. The way you say things matters. So always use a respectful and supportive tone to convey your feedback.

10. Ensure your feedback is based on observable facts and evidence rather than assumptions or hearsay.

11. Strive to be impartial and consider the context before giving feedback.

12. Collaboratively set specific, achievable goals for improvement and discuss how to track progress.

13. And, finally, follow up with the recipient to see how they are progressing and to offer additional support or resources if needed.

Example Phrases for Effective Feedback

Positive Feedback:
- "I really appreciate how you handled the client's concerns yesterday. Your calm and professional demeanor helped resolve the issue quickly."
- "Your presentation was well structured and engaging. The visuals you used made the data easy to understand."

Constructive Feedback:
- "I noticed that there were several errors in the report you submitted last week. Can we review it together to identify areas for improvement?"
- "During our team meetings, it would be helpful if you could let others finish their points before sharing your thoughts. This will ensure everyone feels heard."

Improvement Suggestions:
- "To improve the clarity of your emails, consider using bullet points and short paragraphs. This can help make your messages more readable."
- "Have you thought about taking a course in time management? It could help you manage your workload more effectively."

Feedback-Delivery Frameworks

Powerful feedback-delivery frameworks can also be used to ensure effective coaching feedback:

1. SBI (Situation-Behavior-Impact) Model

One of my go-to methods is the SBI[49] model. It helps provide clear, specific, and constructive feedback by focusing on observable behaviors and their impacts in specific situations.

- **Situation**: Describe the situation where the behavior occurred. This sets the context.

- **Behavior**: Here, you describe the specific behavior you observed. Remember, focus on actions rather than personal attributes.

- **Impact**: Finally, explain the impact of the behavior on you, the team, or the organization. Explain how the behavior affected outcomes or feelings.

    > **Example:** "In yesterday's meeting (**situation**), when you interrupted Peter (**behavior**), it disrupted the flow of the discussion and made it difficult for us to cover all agenda items (**impact**)."

In my own coaching practice, I sometimes like to extend the SBI model to a fourth dimension, that is, the needs of the individual. This allows me to get further commitment on the expected behavior change by engaging the employee to reflect on what support or resources are needed from management, and implicitly committing to use them.

The SBI model is a great approach to use in the context of performance reviews, where feedback on specific actions and their outcomes is needed, but it also works wonders during structured coaching sessions to help individuals understand the

---

[49] The SBI® Model is a registered trademark of the Center for Creative Leadership (CCL). Sloan R. Weitzel, *Feedback That Works: How to Build and Deliver Your Message*, (Center for Creative Leadership, 2000).

effects of their behaviors and identify areas for improvement, and for giving immediate and clear feedback in the context of everyday professional interactions. It's a very effective model and simple enough for everyone to use.

2. DESC (Describe, Express, Specify, Consequences) Model

Another great alternative is the DESC[50] model. It's designed to assertively communicate feedback and address issues, emphasizing both the description of behaviors and the expression of feelings, along with specifying desired changes and outlining potential consequences.

Structure:

- **Describe**: First, you describe the behavior or situation objectively and provide specific details about it.
- **Express**: Then, you express how the behavior or situation makes you feel or the effect it has on others.
- **Specify**: You then specify what you would like to see happen instead, providing clear expectations or desired changes.
- **Consequences**: Finally, you outline the positive outcomes if the change is made or the negative consequences otherwise.

    Example: "During your last few project cycles, I've noticed that the project deadlines weren't met **(describe)**. When deadlines slip, it makes me concerned about the impact on your team's

---

[50] Developed by Sharon Anthony Bower and Gordon H. Bower. See: *Asserting Yourself-Updated Edition: A Practical Guide For Positive Change.* (Da Capo Press, 2004).

performance and your commitments to clients (**express**). I'd like for us to explore strategies together to ensure that you can meet your project deadlines in the future. Perhaps we could look into better time-management tools or prioritize tasks more effectively (**specify**). Ensuring timely project completion is crucial because it helps maintain your team's reputation for reliability and efficiency, and it avoids overloading them with last-minute tasks (**consequences**)."

The DESC model is great for the more "tough love" type of feedback. It's a very effective approach when there is a need to promptly address and resolve conflicts by clearly communicating issues and desired outcomes, or to provide clear and actionable feedback that includes emotional impact and desired changes.

Both the SBI and DESC models are useful tools for providing feedback, but they serve slightly different purposes and contexts. The SBI model is straightforward and ideal for providing clear, objective feedback focused on behavior and its impact, making it useful in performance reviews and coaching. The DESC model is more comprehensive, incorporating emotional expression and specifying desired changes and consequences, making it particularly effective for conflict resolution and assertive communication.

Whatever approach, or combination of approaches, you prefer to use, keep in mind that providing effective and constructive feedback involves being specific, timely, balanced, constructive, respectful, objective, and supportive. Using structured frameworks and positive language helps ensure your feedback is well received and leads to meaningful improvements. And, of course, regular follow-ups and goal setting can further enhance the feedback process, fostering a culture of continuous growth and development.

Encouraging Self-Reflection

Self-reflection is a hugely important part of any type of coaching, both for personal and professional development, particularly where individuals are looking to improve self-awareness, interpersonal skills, and overall effectiveness, which might be the case in a coaching context. The Johari window[51] and reflective journaling techniques are highly effective in structuring this development process.

1. Johari Window

A remarkably simple and effective tool that helps individuals better understand their relationship with themselves and others. It provides insight into what is known and unknown by them and by their peers.

	KNOWN TO SELF	NOT KNOWN TO SELF
KNOWN TO OTHERS	Open Area	Blind Area
NOT KNOWN TO OTHERS	Hidden Area	Unknown Area

>> **Open Area**: Known to oneself and known to others. This includes behaviors, skills, and attitudes that are apparent to both the individual and their peers.

>> **Blind Area**: Known to others but unknown to oneself. This contains things about an individual that others can see but the individual themselves is unaware of.

>> **Hidden Area**: Known to oneself but hidden from others.

---

[51] Joseph Luft and Harrington Ingham, "The Johari window: A graphic model of interpersonal awareness," (1955).

This includes feelings, past experiences, fears, secrets, etc. that an individual chooses not to reveal.

▶▶ **Unknown Area**: Unknown to oneself and others. This quadrant covers latent abilities and feelings that neither the individual nor others are aware of, which could potentially be revealed through deeper reflection and feedback.

The goal in using the Johari window in a coaching context is obviously to increase the open area, thereby enhancing communication, understanding, and effectiveness in personal and professional relationships. By creating a context where our employees feel comfortable enough to be vulnerable, we can encourage them to seek feedback to reduce the blind area, therefore allowing them to learn aspects about themselves that they were previously unaware of. This can improve personal development and effectiveness. Creating an atmosphere of inclusiveness, trust, and respect throughout our organizations can also help employees reveal personal information to reduce the hidden area. This step forward further reinforces trust with others and contributes to improving the employee's interpersonal relationships. Finally, as coaches, we need to support our team members in delving into the unknown area, as it can help them uncover new skills and potentials.

The Johari window aids individuals in understanding themselves better, including how they are perceived by others. By reducing hidden and blind areas, communication can become more open and less inhibited. More importantly, identifying unknown talents and acknowledging weaknesses can lead to better personal and professional growth.

2. Reflective Journaling

Similarly, reflective journaling, when used for self-discovery and improving self-awareness, can be useful as a tool that promotes personal growth, emotional processing, and boosting self-insight. This is because writing down thoughts, feelings, and experiences allows individuals to scale their personal insight, not only as record keeping, but by encouraging respondents to read back and reflect on their own writings, thereby improving their self-awareness. Like the Johari window, reflective journaling can be used to examine both known and unknown aspects of oneself, providing a personal space for self-reflection and discovery.

Reflective journaling facilitates self-reflection in many ways. First, by writing about our own thoughts and feelings on a regular basis, we create the habit of looking inward to make sense of our own actions, choices, and emotional responses. Equally important, journaling may simply offer a safe, private space in which one can vent and let flow a range of feelings that might otherwise remain unacknowledged and unavailable for processing. And this can be particularly therapeutic. It helps individuals process complex feelings, often leading to clarity and resolution. And also, by documenting daily activities and interactions, individuals can observe patterns in their behavior and reactions that may not be evident in the moment. This observation can lead to conscious changes and personal growth.

Combining the Johari window with reflective journaling creates a robust framework for self-reflection. The Johari window's structured feedback mechanism offers external insights, while reflective journaling allows for internal exploration and consolidation of thoughts and emotions. I find that this dual approach ensures a comprehensive understanding of both the individual's perceived and actual self, which can lead to significant personal growth and increased self-awareness.

Strength-Based Approach to Feedback and Coaching

As a strong advocate for competency-based management, I am particularly keen on implementing a strength-based approach to feedback and coaching. This approach, commonly associated with the work of Donald O. Clifton and colleagues at Gallup, focuses on identifying and leveraging an individual's strengths and talents rather than solely addressing their weaknesses or areas for improvement. It aims to build on what individuals do well to enhance their performance, engagement, and overall satisfaction. After all, would you ask a person of short stature to change the light bulbs around the building, knowing they will always have to drag around a ladder? Or would you ask a taller person to do so instead? Similarly, why not focus on developing employees' natural strengths, identifying initially what each individual will be a rock star at? Isn't this a better use of your training and development budget? That's what the strength-based approach is all about, and it is articulated around a few key principles:

- The need to emphasize positive aspects of performance and character.
- The need to encourage individuals to use their strengths to overcome challenges.
- The need to foster a mindset that focuses on continuous learning and development.
- The need to engage individuals by aligning their tasks and roles with their strengths.
- The need to build sustainable performance improvements by reinforcing what individuals naturally do well.

To be implemented effectively, this approach needs to be structured around a couple of important pillars:

1. Strengths identification: Use assessment tools to identify individual strengths and encourage individuals to reflect on past successes and identify the skills and behaviors that contributed to those successes. We also have to gather feedback from peers, managers, and colleagues to gain a well-rounded view of an individual's strengths. Instruments such as 360-degree feedback are, of course, ideal in this situation.

2. Strengths-based feedback: Provide specific and detailed feedback on what the individual did well, explain how their strengths contributed to positive outcomes and success, and encourage them to continue using their strengths in similar or new situations.

   Example: "Your ability to analyze data quickly and accurately was instrumental in completing the project ahead of schedule. This strength in analytical thinking is a major asset to our team."

3. Strengths-based goal setting: Set goals that allow individuals to use their strengths regularly and identify areas where strengths can be applied to address challenges or areas for development.

   Example: "Let's set a goal for you to lead the next data-analysis project, leveraging your strong analytical skills to enhance our reporting process."

4. Strength-oriented development plans: Create development plans that focus on enhancing and expanding the use of strengths and provide opportunities for learning and growth that align with the individual's strengths.

> Example: "To further develop your analytical skills, we can arrange for advanced data-analytics training and give you more opportunities to lead complex projects."

5. Strengths-oriented coaching conversations: Structure coaching conversations to highlight strengths and explore how they can be used to achieve goals. And while focusing on strengths, we also have to address areas for improvement in a constructive manner, showing how strengths can help overcome these areas.

   > Example: "You've shown great initiative in leading projects, and your strong organizational skills really shine. Let's also work on your presentation skills so you can share your insights more effectively with the team."

Don't take my word for it—ask any organization that has adopted this approach. The outcomes speak for themselves. Individuals are generally more engaged and motivated when they are able to use their strengths regularly. Focusing on strengths leads to better performance and higher productivity. Individuals experience higher job satisfaction when their work aligns with their strengths. Teams that leverage the strengths of their members tend to be more cohesive and effective. And building on strengths generally leads to more sustainable personal and professional growth.

By identifying, utilizing, and developing individual strengths, we can foster a positive and empowering environment that drives engagement, performance, and satisfaction. Through specific and strengths-focused feedback, aligned goal setting, and tailored development plans, the strength-based approach creates a foundation for continuous improvement and success.

Developing Active Listening

Developing active-listening skills is crucial for effective communication, especially in performance coaching and feedback. Active listening involves fully concentrating on, understanding, responding to, and remembering what is being said. Here are practical steps to develop and enhance your active-listening skills:

1. Give the team member your undivided attention. That means avoiding distractions such as phones, computers, or side conversations. Maintaining appropriate eye contact demonstrates that you are focused and interested. And it's important to pay attention to the employee's body language, facial expressions, and tone of voice, as these can provide additional context to their words.

2. Use facial expressions and body language to show that you are listening and understanding. And use brief verbal acknowledgments like "I see," "I understand," or "Go on" to encourage the individual to continue.

3. Learn to summarize what an employee says in your own words to confirm understanding, while reflecting on their feelings or emotions. For instance, "It sounds like you're feeling frustrated about the situation."

4. Let the other person finish their thoughts without interruption to show respect and allow for a complete understanding of their perspective. All while keeping an open mind and avoiding jumping to conclusions or making judgments before they have finished.

5. Make good use of open-ended questions to clarify and delve deeper into their points. For example, "Can you tell me more about that?" It's also essential to offer thoughtful and constructive feedback based on what you've heard. Your responses should always be relevant and considerate. And most importantly, you need to show empathy by acknowledging their feelings and experiences. For instance, "I can understand why that would be challenging."

6. But you also need to stay present in the moment, fully concentrating on the individual and their message without letting your mind wander. Use deep-breathing techniques to stay calm and focused during the conversation.

7. Remain aware of your own emotions and how they might affect your listening, and cultivate empathy by trying to understand their perspective and emotions.

8. Don't hesitate to ask colleagues, friends, or family members for feedback on your listening skills. Reflect on that feedback and work on the specific areas identified for improvement.

9. And finally, take your own medicine. You need to regularly engage in conversations where you can practice active listening, in both professional and personal contexts. And practice active listening through role-playing exercises, as this can help simulate real-life scenarios and improve your skills in a safe environment.

Practice, practice, and practice some more! There's no secret. For us coaches, it's a must-have that we need to continuously hone through time, practice, and efforts. And if you are still learning to become an active listener, try some simple developmental exercises. Try this simple one-minute drill: Spend one minute fully listening to someone speak without interrupting. After they finish, summarize what they said to ensure you understood correctly. Keep a journal of your listening experiences, where you note situations where you practiced active listening and reflect on what went well and what could be improved. Participate in listening circles or groups where the primary focus is on developing and practicing active-listening skills. Be creative and get exposed! By consistently practicing these techniques and being mindful of your listening habits, you can develop strong active-listening skills that enhance communication and improve your relationships in both personal and professional settings.

Asking Open-Ended Questions

A few years ago, I got involved in training individuals and groups in evidence-based coaching. One of the most difficult aspects of this was teaching people how to ask questions. I mean good questions. Questions that open the door to valuable and actionable insights. I realized that this does not necessarily come naturally, even, surprisingly enough, to experienced coaches. Open-ended questions are designed to encourage a full, meaningful answer using the subject's own knowledge and feelings. They are a critical tool in coaching, feedback, and many other communication contexts.

In a nutshell, open-ended questions are questions that cannot be answered with a simple "yes" or "no" or with a specific piece of information. They require the respondent to elaborate on their thoughts, feelings, or experiences. And they serve the purpose of encouraging deeper conversation and insight, gathering detailed information, fostering creative thinking and problem-solving, and, of course, building rapport and understanding.

Open-ended questions often begin with "what," "how," "why," or "tell me about . . ." These starters naturally prompt more detailed responses, and they invite the respondent to explain, describe, or reflect. But most importantly, they require more than one-word answers.

So, how do we go about asking open-ended questions?

1. It may sound obvious, but still, we should understand why we are asking the question in the first place. Are we seeking information, clarification, or encouraging self-reflection?

2. Avoid like the plague starters that lead to yes-or-no answers like "is," "are," "do," or "did."

3. Ensure the question is clear and focused. That means not too broad or vague, as this can confuse the respondent.

4. We also need to approach the question with genuine curiosity and an open mind, so it's best to steer clear of questions that may sound judgmental or leading.

5. And finally, follow up with additional open-ended questions or prompts, especially when the initial response is brief. Appropriating and adapting the rationale of the trusted Toyota's 5 Whys technique[52] can be useful here.

Examples of Open-Ended Questions

General Conversations:

▶▶ "What are your thoughts on . . . ?"

▶▶ "How do you feel about . . . ?"

---

[52] Taiichi Ohno, *Toyota Production System: Beyond Large-Scale Production* (Productivity Press, 1988).

- "Can you describe your experience with . . . ?"
- "What challenges have you faced with . . . ?"

Coaching and Feedback:
- "What do you think went well during the project?"
- "How did you approach the problem?"
- "Why do you think that strategy worked?"
- "Tell me about a time when you felt most engaged at work."

Problem-Solving:
- "What are some possible solutions you see for this issue?"
- "How would you approach this challenge differently next time?"
- "What factors do you think contributed to this outcome?"
- "Why do you believe this is the best course of action?"

Self-Reflection:
- "What have you learned from this experience?"
- "How has this situation affected your perspective?"
- "Why is this goal important to you?"
- "What are your biggest strengths and how do you use them?"

When trying to ask good open-ended questions, give the respondent time to think and elaborate on their answer. Show that you are engaged and interested in their response by using your active-listening skills. Let the respondent complete their thoughts without interruption and use follow-up questions to delve deeper based on their responses: "Can you tell me more about that?" or "What happened next?" By all means, avoid leading questions that imply a right or wrong answer. And don't forget to encourage the respondent to share stories and examples as this often provides richer, more detailed information.

⩓

Helping Team Members Set Boundaries

Ensuring an employee can set boundaries effectively is crucial for maintaining a healthy work-life balance and preventing burnout. The following guidelines can help them set and maintain boundaries:

1. Encourage the individual to list their professional and personal priorities. Understanding what is most important to them can help in setting clear boundaries. It's necessary to help them recognize early signs of burnout, such as constant fatigue, lack of motivation, or irritability. Self-awareness is the first step in establishing healthy boundaries.

2. Advise them to establish clear start and end times for their workday, and encourage them to stick to these hours as much as possible. They should take regular breaks throughout the day to rest and recharge. This can include short breaks, lunch breaks, and stepping away from work during weekends or days off. It's also important to teach them to use time blocking to allocate specific times for focused work, meetings, and personal time. This helps in managing their time more effectively and preventing work from spilling into personal time.

3. Encourage the individual to communicate their boundaries clearly to colleagues and supervisors; for example, letting others know their preferred working hours and when they are available for meetings or calls. Teach them to politely decline additional tasks or projects when they are already at capacity. This can be done by explaining their current workload and suggesting alternative solutions or timelines. It's also necessary to recommend setting boundaries with communication tools, such as turning off work-related notifications after working hours and using separate devices for work and personal use if possible.

4. If working remotely, advise the individual to create a dedicated workspace that is separate from their living space. This physical boundary can help in mentally separating work from personal life. And we need to suggest establishing daily rituals to signal the start and end of the workday, such as a morning routine before work and a wind-down routine after work.

5. Encourage them also to set personal goals that are separate from work. This can include hobbies, fitness goals, or learning new skills. Having personal goals helps in maintaining a balanced life. We should advise them to seek support from mentors, coaches, or support groups if they find it challenging to set boundaries. Sometimes, talking to others who have successfully managed similar challenges can provide valuable insights.

6. And finally, it's essential to emphasize the importance of self-care practices such as regular exercise, adequate sleep, healthy eating, and relaxation techniques. These practices can improve overall well-being and resilience. We can recommend mindfulness practices, such as

meditation or yoga, to help them stay present and manage stress more effectively.

Example Conversations and Scripts

Setting Expectations with Colleagues:
"I wanted to let you know that my work hours are from nine a.m. to five p.m. If you need anything urgent outside of these hours, please send me an email, and I will address it the next working day."

Politely Declining Additional Work:
"I appreciate the opportunity to take on this project. However, my current workload doesn't allow me to commit fully at the moment. Could we discuss a possible timeline extension or delegation of tasks?"

Communicating Break Times:
"I take a lunch break from noon to one every day. I won't be available during this time, but I will respond to any messages as soon as I return."

Recommending these strategies can help us ensure that team members establish and maintain effective boundaries, leading to better work-life balance, increased productivity, and overall well-being. Providing continuous support and feedback will further empower them to stick to their boundaries and make necessary adjustments as needed.

Understanding Learning Styles

One of the ways to make performance coaching more effective is to appreciate the wide range of learning styles. When you recognize each employee's learning style, you're better equipped to overcome their barriers to learning through more meaningful one-on-one conversations. Besides being able to communicate better, you'll also help them retain information faster, and you'll keep them more engaged and motivated.

Here's a comprehensive overview of several prominent learning-style theories and their practical applications.

1. Gregorc's Mind Styles Model[53]

Anthony F. Gregorc developed the Mind Styles Model in the 1970s, focusing on how individuals perceive and order information. Gregorc identified two perceptual qualities (concrete and abstract) and two ordering abilities (sequential and random), resulting in four learning styles: Concrete Sequential, Abstract Sequential, Abstract Random, and Concrete Random. This model emphasizes the importance of cognitive preferences in learning.

Learning Styles:

- Concrete Sequential (CS): Prefers structured, sequential information and hands-on activities.

- Abstract Sequential (AS): Prefers theoretical, logical information presented in a structured way.

- Abstract Random (AR): Prefers unstructured, intuitive information and personal connections.

- Concrete Random (CR): Prefers hands-on, trial-and-error approaches and spontaneous activities.

---

[53] Anthony F. Gregorc, *The Mind Styles Model: Theories, Principles, and Applications* (2006).

Practical Applications:

▶▶ Concrete Sequential: Provide detailed instructions, schedules, and step-by-step tasks.

▶▶ Abstract Sequential: Use lectures, readings, and logical explanations.

▶▶ Abstract Random: Encourage group discussions, personal reflections, and flexibility.

▶▶ Concrete Random: Facilitate hands-on experiments, brainstorming sessions, and creative projects.

2. VARK Model[54]

In the late 1980s psychologist Neil D. Fleming came up with the VARK model of learning styles—Visual, Aural, Read/Write, and Kinesthetic—in an attempt to elucidate the distinct learning styles of different people. Its popularity rests upon the claim that, by becoming aware of their preferred learning styles, both teachers and students can process information more efficiently and effectively. Ultimately, this model suggests, learning will be maximized if you appreciate that different people learn in different ways. And, if it works in the classroom, there are definitely elements we can apply to our coaching interventions.

Learning Styles:

▶▶ Visual: prefers using images, diagrams, and spatial understanding.

▶▶ Aural: prefers listening to information and engaging in discussions.

---

[54] "VARK® Modalities: What do Visual, Aural, Read/write & Kinesthetic really mean?" VARK Learn Limited, accessed March 7, 2025, https://vark-learn.com/introduction-to-vark/the-vark-modalities/.

- ▶▶ Read/Write: prefers reading texts and writing notes.
- ▶▶ Kinesthetic: prefers hands-on experiences and learning by doing.

Practical Applications:

- ▶▶ Visual: Use charts, graphs, and color-coded notes. Encourage the use of visual aids in presentations.
- ▶▶ Aural: Provide lectures, podcasts, and opportunities for group discussions. Use mnemonic devices and verbal repetition.
- ▶▶ Read/Write: Supply plenty of reading materials, encourage note-taking, and provide written instructions and reports.
- ▶▶ Kinesthetic: Incorporate hands-on activities, experiments, and physical demonstrations. Use role-playing and real-world simulations.

3. Multiple Intelligences Theory[55]

Howard Gardner introduced the theory of multiple intelligences in the excellent 1983 book *Frames of Mind: The Theory of Multiple Intelligences*. Gardner proposed that traditional notions of intelligence, as measured by IQ tests, were too limited. Instead, he identified eight distinct types of intelligences that people possess to varying degrees. This theory has broad implications for education and coaching, suggesting that coaching methods should be diversified to cater to the various intelligences present in a room.

---

[55] Howard Gardner, *Frames of Mind: The Theory of Multiple Intelligences*, (Basic Books, 2011).

Types of Intelligences:
- Linguistic: Sensitivity to spoken and written language.
- Logical-Mathematical: Ability to think logically and solve mathematical problems.
- Spatial: Ability to visualize and manipulate objects in space.
- Musical: Skill in performing, composing, and appreciating musical patterns.
- Bodily-Kinesthetic: Using the body to solve problems or create products.
- Interpersonal: Understanding and interacting with others.
- Intrapersonal: Understanding oneself.
- Naturalist: Recognizing and categorizing natural objects.

Practical Applications:
- Linguistic: Use storytelling, debates, and writing assignments.
- Logical-Mathematical: Provide puzzles, problem-solving tasks, and experiments.
- Spatial: Utilize visual arts, models, and graphic organizers.
- Musical: Incorporate music, rhythm, and instruments in learning activities.
- Bodily-Kinesthetic: Engage in physical activities and hands-on learning.
- Interpersonal: Facilitate group work, peer tutoring, and social activities.

- Intrapersonal: Encourage self-reflection, journaling, and goal setting.

- Naturalist: Use nature walks, field trips, and studies of the natural world.

4. Kolb's Experiential Learning Theory[56]

David A Kolb's Experiential Learning Theory provides a more contemporary model for learning, which posits that knowledge is created through the transformation of experience. According to this model, the learning cycle moves through four different stages: Concrete Experience (feelings), Reflective Observation (experience), Abstract Conceptualization (thought), and Active Experimentation (doing). In addition, Kolb outlines four learning styles based on people's preferences for certain stages of the cycle.

Learning Styles:

- Concrete Experience (CE): Learning through direct experience.

- Reflective Observation (RO): Learning by reflecting on experiences.

- Abstract Conceptualization (AC): Learning through logical analysis and planning.

- Active Experimentation (AE): Learning by testing theories and applying knowledge.

Practical Applications:

- Concrete Experience: Use simulations, fieldwork, and hands-on projects.

---

[56] David A. Kolb, *Experiential Learning: Experience as the Source of Learning and Development*, 2nd ed. (Pearson Education, Inc., 2015).

- ▶ Reflective Observation: Encourage discussions, journaling, and reviewing case studies.

- ▶ Abstract Conceptualization: Provide lectures, readings, and model building.

- ▶ Active Experimentation: Facilitate role-playing, experiments, and real-world problem-solving.

5. Honey and Mumford Learning Styles[57]

Another broad model was developed by Peter Honey and Alan Mumford and based on David Kolb's work. Their learning styles model attempts to identify four distinct styles that can be applied in learning. This model also helps identify which learning style suits an individual by suggesting that good learning should address one's strengths and weaknesses. Honey and Mumford's four styles are Activist, Reflector, Theorist, and Pragmatist.

Learning Styles:

- ▶ Activist: Learners who enjoy new experiences and challenges.

- ▶ Reflector: Learners who like to observe and reflect on experiences.

- ▶ Theorist: Learners who prefer to understand the theory behind actions.

- ▶ Pragmatist: Learners who are keen to apply new ideas practically.

Practical Applications:

- ▶ Activist: Use brainstorming sessions, games, and role-playing.

---

[57] Honey, P., & Mumford, A. (1986). The Manual of Learning Styles. Peter Honey Publications.

- **Reflector:** Provide opportunities for observation, diaries, and feedback sessions.
- **Theorist:** Include models, concepts, and logical explanations.
- **Pragmatist:** Offer practical tasks, case studies, and simulations.

	Gregorc's Mind Styles Model	VARK Model	Multiple Intelligences Theory	Kolb's Experiential Learning Theory	Honey and Mumford Learning Styles
Developer	Anthony F. Gregorc	Neil D. Fleming	Howard Gardner	David A. Kolb	Peter Honey and Alan Mumford
Focus	Cognitive preferences in perceiving and ordering information	Sensory modalities of learning	Diverse intelligences	Learning through experience	Learning preferences based on behavior
Learning Styles/ Types	Concrete Sequential, Abstract Sequential, Abstract Random, Concrete Random	Visual, Aural/Auditory, Read/Write, Kinesthetic	Linguistic, Logical-Mathematical, Spatial, Musical, Bodily-Kinesthetic, Interpersonal, Intrapersonal, Naturalist	Concrete Experience, Reflective Observation, Abstract Conceptualization, Active Experimentation	Activist, Reflector, Theorist, Pragmatist

Key Principles	Individuals have distinct ways of perceiving and ordering information. Cognitive preferences influence learning and behavior.	Different people prefer different sensory modalities for learning. Matching teaching methods to these preferences can enhance learning.	Intelligence is not a single entity but consists of multiple types. Individuals possess varying levels of different intelligences.	Learning is a cyclic process involving four stages. Effective learning integrates all four stages.	Learning styles are based on behavior. Individuals prefer different approaches to learning based on their personality and experience.
Strengths	Highlights the importance of cognitive processes. Provides insights into personal learning preferences.	Easy to understand and apply. Provides clear strategies for different learning preferences.	Recognizes diverse talents and abilities. Promotes a more inclusive approach to learning.	Emphasizes the importance of experience in learning. Adaptable to various professional contexts.	Practical and easy to apply. Focuses on real-world learning applications.
Limitations	May be too rigid in categorizing cognitive styles. Not widely adopted or recognized.	Can oversimplify learning preferences. Does not account for the complexity of cognitive processes.	Can be challenging to implement in traditional coaching settings. May require significant resources and adjustments.	Can be complex to understand and apply. May not account for all individual learning preferences.	Can be seen as an extension of Kolb's theory. May not cover all aspects of learning.
Applications	Adapting teaching and training methods.	Training and development programs.	Personal and professional development.	Personal and professional development.	Enhancing training and development.

Understanding and applying these learning styles can create more effective and engaging coaching experiences. Recognizing that individuals may have preferences for certain styles or a combination of them allows for a more personalized approach to teaching and learning, ultimately enhancing comprehension and knowledge retention. Each of these theories offers unique insights into how people learn, providing valuable frameworks to cater to diverse learning needs.

Instruments-Based Assessments

Understanding the differences, strengths, and limitations of various feedback and evaluation methods can help organizations choose the most appropriate approach for their needs. That is, if used properly. All instruments-based assessment processes should follow two critical rules.

First, prior to the implementation of any assessment, the concerned employee needs to understand the purpose of the assessment, what's being measured, the possible consequences, how the results will be used, and what form of output they should anticipate. Second, once the assessment is complete, it needs to be materialized for the employee as a tangible output. Basically, if the employee has committed time and effort to complete the questionnaire, then they should receive something in return, be it in the form of a personalized results report, a group feedback session, or a one-on-one results-interpretation session for results that might be more complex to analyze.

Failure to follow either of these rules could result in collected data that is invalid or inaccurate. Indeed, employees may fear the consequences of assessments, particularly how their results will be used by the organization. This fear could lead them to manipulate outcomes or answer dishonestly. For example, they might provide answers they think are expected rather than ones that reflect their true selves, which certainly undermines the validity and usability of assessment results intended to support their development.

The most commonly used methodologies, namely, 360-degree feedback, self-assessment, and peer evaluation, are discussed below.

1. 360-Degree Feedback

360-degree feedback involves collecting feedback from a variety of sources, including supervisors, peers, subordinates, and sometimes even customers. This comprehensive approach provides a well-rounded view of an individual's performance and behaviors.

Components:
- Feedback from multiple sources (supervisors, peers, subordinates, self, and sometimes customers).
- Usually involves structured surveys or questionnaires.
- Focuses on competencies, behaviors, and performance.

Strengths:
- Holistic view: Provides a comprehensive picture of an individual's performance from multiple perspectives.
- Improved self-awareness: Helps individuals understand how they are perceived by others.
- Balanced feedback: Reduces bias by incorporating diverse viewpoints.
- Development focus: Primarily used for personal and professional growth rather than evaluation.

Limitations:

▶▶ Complexity: Can be time-consuming and complex to administer and analyze.

▶▶ Potential for bias: Anonymity may lead to less accountability for feedback.

▶▶ Resistance: Some individuals may be resistant to receiving feedback from peers and subordinates.

Best Used For:

▶▶ Leadership development

▶▶ Comprehensive performance reviews

▶▶ Identifying blind spots and areas for development

2. Self-Assessment

Self-assessment involves individuals evaluating their own performance and behaviors. This method encourages self-reflection and self-awareness. Various tools can be used in this context such as personality inventories, like the Myers-Briggs Type Indicator (MBTI), the DiSC[58] assessment, and the gazillions of instruments based on the Big Five model[59] of personality, but also emotional intelligence instruments, and other skills and competency Assessments.

Components:

▶▶ Personal reflection and evaluation

▶▶ Self-assessment forms or questionnaires

▶▶ Setting personal goals and identifying areas for improvement

---

[58] William M. Marston, *Emotions of Normal People* (Harcourt, Brace & World, 1928).

[59] P. T. Costa and R. R. McCrae, "A five-factor theory of personality," in *Handbook of personality: Theory and research*, eds. L. A. Pervin and O. P. John (Guilford Press, 1999), 139–153.

Strengths:

» Self-awareness: Encourages individuals to reflect on their own preferences, strengths, and weaknesses.

» Empowerment: Involves individuals in their own development process, promoting ownership and accountability.

» Simple to implement: Easy to administer without the need for extensive resources.

Limitations:

» Bias: Individuals may overestimate or underestimate their performance.

» Lack of external perspective: Does not provide insights from others, potentially missing key areas for improvement.

» Honesty: Requires individuals to be honest and objective about their own performance.

Best Used For:

» Personal-development planning

» Supplementing other feedback methods

» Initial stages of performance reviews

3. Peer Evaluation

Peer evaluation involves colleagues at the same hierarchical level providing feedback on each other's performance and behaviors. This method leverages the insights of those who work closely with the individual.

Components:

- Feedback from peers and colleagues
- Structured forms or informal feedback sessions
- Focuses on collaboration, teamwork, and specific competencies

Strengths:

- Relevant feedback: Peers often have a clear understanding of an individual's day-to-day performance and interactions.
- Improved team dynamics: Can enhance mutual respect and understanding within a team.
- Specific insights: Provides detailed insights into collaborative and interpersonal skills.

Limitations:

- Bias and favoritism: May be influenced by personal relationships and biases.
- Reluctance: Peers may be reluctant to provide negative feedback due to fear of damaging relationships.
- Limited scope: Does not provide a comprehensive view, as it lacks input from supervisors and subordinates.

Best Used For:

- Enhancing teamwork and collaboration
- Providing feedback on interpersonal skills
- Supplementing supervisor evaluations

4. Pulse Surveys

Pulse surveys are short and frequent surveys that capture real-time feedback about a specific issue within the organization. They might be particularly interesting when it comes to measuring the immediate effects of a new initiative or structural changes inside an organization—for example, how the organization is perceived by colleagues after an infrastructure upgrade. The questions covered are quite simple and short, thus making the frequent distribution of such surveys feasible.

Components:

- Regular and frequent deployment: Surveys are sent out on a regular basis (e.g., weekly, monthly).

- Focused content: Questions are concise and targeted to specific topics of immediate relevance.

- Quick to complete: Designed to be completed in a few minutes to encourage high response rates.

Strengths:

- Timeliness: Provides immediate feedback, allowing for quick reactions to any arising issues.

- High response rates: The brevity and frequency encourage more employees to participate.

- Continuous feedback: Offers ongoing insights into the health of the organization, making it easier to track trends over time.

Limitations:

- Surface-level insights: Due to their brevity, pulse surveys may not provide deep insights into complex issues.

▶▶ Survey fatigue: Despite being brief, the frequency can lead to disengagement if not managed properly.

▶▶ Dependency on question quality: The effectiveness of the feedback relies heavily on the relevance and quality of the questions asked.

Best Used For:

▶▶ Monitoring the impact of recent changes or initiatives

▶▶ Quickly assessing employee sentiment and morale

▶▶ Complementing deeper, more comprehensive annual surveys

Each feedback method—360-degree feedback, self-assessment, peer evaluation, and pulse surveys—has its unique advantages and limitations. The choice of method should be based on the specific goals and context of the feedback process. Often, a combination of these methods can provide a more balanced and effective approach to performance evaluation and development. Each of these assessment methods offers unique insights into different aspects of an individual's performance, behavior, and personality. By using these tools, team members can gain a deeper understanding of their strengths and areas for improvement, set meaningful goals, and develop targeted action plans for personal and professional growth.

⚠

Competency Assessments Versus Personality Tests

What about when you want to assist an employee and you're not sure whether you should use an assessment that measures competencies or one that measures personality? It's the equivalent of being asked if you'd like chocolate or vanilla ice cream... You like them both, yet they satisfy different cravings!

Let's chat about these two coaching tools and how they can spice up your coaching game. First up, competency assessments. These act as your trusty GPS for skill development. I recall one time I was working with a brilliant sales associate who wanted to move into sales management. We used a predictive competency assessment, and boom! We discovered he had killer sales skills but needed to work on his people-management abilities.

Competency assessments are your go-to tool when you're dealing with:

- Skill gaps (like that sales associate's management skills)
- Career transitions (ever tried to leap from marketing to finance without a road map?)
- Team building (because let's face it, a team full of idea people but no executors is a recipe for disaster)

Now, turning over to personality tests. These are like having a backstage pass to someone's mind. They're great for initiating those "aha" moments when an employee finally understands why he and his coworkers butt heads or what drains him about giving presentations.

I remember working with James, a high-flying executive in Singapore who couldn't figure out why he was constantly having disagreements with his team. One of my personality tests (based on the Big Five model) revealed he was a hardcore introvert trying to lead like an extrovert. Once we figured that out, it was like someone had turned on the lights!

Personality tests shine when you're tackling:

- Self-awareness (because sometimes we're the last to know our own quirks)

- ▶▶ Leadership styles (ever seen a drill sergeant try to lead a team of creatives? not pretty)
- ▶▶ Team dynamics (it's like solving a human puzzle)

Yet, it's not an either-or scenario—you can use both! And many of us do in our practices. You get to see not just what someone is capable of, but also how they're likely to do it. For example, on the sales team I once coached, we administered competency assessments to identify who needed to improve their closing techniques but also personality tests to understand their natural communication styles. The result? We could tailor their training to not just improve their skills, but to do so in a way that felt natural to them. Talk about a win-win!

Now, I need to be honest and admit that, while I do use many different personality tests in my coaching practice, I have a stronger preference for competency assessments. And to justify that position, I have to wear my academic hat (I work with clients as an organizational-development consultant and coach, yet, I'm also a university professor) and revert to the basics of Kurt Lewin's formula $B = f(P, E)$, or in simple terms: Behavior is a function of the Person and their Environment. Plain and simple: Competency assessments generally have better predictive validity and reliability compared to personality tests for several reasons, particularly when it comes to workplace performance and specific job-related behaviors. Here's why:

1. Relevance to job performance: Competency assessments are tailored to evaluate specific job-related competencies, such as technical skills, leadership abilities, or communication effectiveness. The questions are designed to reflect real-world scenarios an employee might encounter on the job, making the assessment

highly relevant to actual work performance. On the other hand, personality tests, while they provide valuable insights into an individual's traits and general behavioral tendencies, are not specifically designed to measure job-related skills. Instead, they assess broader personality characteristics which may influence behavior but are not direct indicators of job performance.

2. Predictive validity: Competency assessments, by focusing on specific competencies that are essential for success in a given role, have strong predictive validity. They can accurately forecast an individual's ability to perform job functions because they measure directly applicable skills and knowledge. Personality tests tend to have lower predictive validity for job performance because they measure more general and stable traits that influence behavior in a wide variety of contexts, not just at work.

3. Susceptibility to response bias: While competency assessments are still self-report instruments (but 360-degree versions exist) and can be subject to some bias, the specific nature of the questions (often related to observable actions and decisions) can help mitigate the extent of bias, as responses are easier to verify against actual job performance. Personality tests are more susceptible to response biases such as social desirability or self-deceptive positivity. Participants may respond based on how they wish to be perceived rather than provide an accurate self-assessment.

4. Use in organizational settings: Finally, competency assessments are ideal for performance evaluations, identifying training needs, and guiding career-development paths. They provide actionable data that can directly influence personnel decisions and development strategies.

On the other hand, personality tests are best used for understanding team dynamics, enhancing workplace communication, and informing recruitment by providing a broader view of potential employee fit within team cultures or roles that require specific personality traits.

Competency assessments are more directly aligned with evaluating and enhancing job performance, offering high specificity and direct applicability to job tasks. They are effective tools for performance management and training within organizational settings. Personality tests, while offering broad insights into an individual's behavioral tendencies, do not directly assess job-specific skills and are less predictive of job performance, making them more suitable for roles in team placement and cultural integration. In simple terms, "if personality traits tell you how someone prefers to work, only competencies show you what they can actually accomplish . . ." as rightfully pointed out by my team at ProfilAS[60].

There's no doubt that both are indeed useful, and both serve their function well. But since performance coaching is all about efficiently pinpointing and addressing performance on the job, I find competency assessments more precise with results reliable over much longer periods.

Behavioral-Observation Template for Performance Coaching

In shadowing, the coach accompanies the employee into their natural work environment (and usually, for a set period of time).

---

[60] Founded by Dr. Behar-Courtois in 2024, ProfilAS is a talent-analytics company whose unique approach combines research-validated psychometrics and AI technology to create predictive competency assessments that transform how organizations recruit, develop, and manage their employees. See: https://profilas.com

The essence is to observe the employee in action, watching and listening to how they engage with others and handle their daily workload and tasks. The aim is to pick up, in situ, insights into effective ways in which the employee operates, the underlying assumptions that drive their behavior, the recurring issues they are facing, the matters that trip them up, and where—in the eye of the coach—they might be able to raise their game. The idea here is to use shadowing to spot, pinpoint, and hone in on the areas that are crucial to lay the basis for more focused and effective coaching. Following is a simple template I like to use in the context of shadowing sessions with clients.

Observer Information	
Observer Name:	Date of Observation:
Location:	Time of Observation:

Coachee Information	
Name:	Role/Position:
Department/Team:	

Observation Context	
Type of Activity/Task:	Duration of Observation:
Objective of Activity/Task:	

Behavior Observation

Behavior Being Observed:

Operational Definition *(clearly define the behavior in observable and measurable terms)*:

Frequency and Duration

Number of Occurrences:

Total Duration of Behavior:

Frequency:

Antecedents

Events/Conditions Before Behavior:

Behavior Description

Detailed Description of Behavior:

Consequences

Events/Conditions After Behavior:

Environmental Context

Physical Environment *(e.g., workspace setup, noise level)*:

Social Context

Interactions with Others *(e.g., interactions with colleagues, supervisors)*:

Qualitative Notes

Additional Observations *(any other relevant information or context)*:

Behavior Analysis

Pattern Identification

Patterns Noted in Behavior:

Potential Triggers

Possible Antecedents/Triggers:

Function of Behavior

Hypothesized Function *(e.g., seeking attention, avoiding tasks, demonstrating competence)*:

Impact on Performance

Positive Impacts:

Negative Impacts:

Feedback and Action Plan	
Strengths Identified:	Areas for Improvement:

Recommended Actions

Short-Term Actions:	Long-Term Actions:

Support Needed

Resources or Training:	Mentorship or Guidance:

Follow-Up Plan	
Next Observation Date:	Next Coaching-Session Date:
Metrics for Success:	

An easier way to perhaps understand how to use this template is through an example:

Observer Information	
Observer Name: Dr. Behar-Courtois	Date of Observation: May 10, 2024
Location: office workspace	Time of Observation: 9:00 a.m. – 10:00 a.m.
Coachee Information	
Name: Rachel Green	Role/Position: Project Manager
Department/Team: IT Development Team	
Observation Context	
Type of Activity/Task: project-planning meeting	Duration of Observation: 1 hour
Objective of Activity/Task: Develop a project timeline and assign tasks to team members	

Behavior Observation
Behavior Being Observed: Effective delegation and team engagement
Operational Definition *(clearly define the behavior in observable and measurable terms)*:
Clearly assigning tasks to team members, ensuring everyone understands their responsibilities, and fostering engagement through active participation
Frequency and Duration
Number of Occurrences: 4
Total Duration of Behavior: 20 minutes
Frequency: Delegated tasks in 4 distinct instances
Antecedents
Events/Conditions Before Behavior:
Review of project objectives, initial discussion of team roles

Behavior Description

Detailed Description of Behavior:

Rachel reviewed the project objectives, assigned specific tasks to team members, asked for feedback, and encouraged questions to ensure understanding.

Consequences

Events/Conditions After Behavior:

Team members expressed clarity on their tasks, engaged in the discussion, and provided input on task timelines.

Environmental Context

Physical Environment *(e.g., workspace setup, noise level)*:

Open-plan office, conference table, moderate noise level

Social Context

Interactions with Others *(e.g., interactions with colleagues, supervisors)*:

Positive and collaborative interactions with team members, active listening, and respectful communication

Qualitative Notes

Additional Observations *(any other relevant information or context)*:

Rachel maintained a positive and encouraging tone, which contributed to team members' willingness to participate and share their ideas.

Behavior Analysis

Pattern Identification

Patterns Noted in Behavior:

Consistent clarity in communication, effective task delegation, and active encouragement of team participation

Potential Triggers

Possible Antecedents/Triggers:

Clear project objectives, supportive team environment

Function of Behavior

Hypothesized Function *(e.g., seeking attention, avoiding tasks, demonstrating competence)*:

Ensuring project success through clear delegation and fostering a collaborative team environment

Impact on Performance

Positive Impacts:

Improved team clarity and engagement, efficient task allocation

Negative Impacts:

None observed

Feedback and Action Plan

Strengths Identified:	Areas for Improvement:
Strong delegation skills	Could enhance time management to ensure all agenda items are covered within the meeting time
Effective team engagement and communication	

Recommended Actions

Short-Term Actions:	Long-Term Actions:
Implement a meeting agenda with time allocations for each item	Provide training on advanced time-management techniques

Support Needed

Resources or Training:	Mentorship or Guidance:
Training on time management and effective meeting facilitation	Regular check-ins with a senior project manager to discuss time-management strategies

Follow-Up Plan

Next Observation Date: May 17, 2024	Next Coaching-Session Date: May 20, 2024

Metrics for Success:

Improved time management in meetings

Continued effective delegation and team engagement

Stay Versus Exit Interviews

Both stay and exit interviews complement each other beautifully. Stay interviews help companies prevent issues, while exit interviews help companies understand what they missed and how to do better next time.

1. Stay Interviews

Imagine you're in a relationship. You don't wait for your significant other to stick a suitcase in the back of their car and start the ignition before you ask what's going on, do you? That's the beauty of the stay interview; it's simply a conversation you have with your existing employees to find out what motivates them and what might make them . . . cease being motivated.

So, what exactly are stay interviews? They're structured, one-on-one conversations between a manager and an employee that are designed to gauge levels of engagement, and to identify and potentially act on problems or underlying issues. In short, they determine job satisfaction. It's about asking, "What makes you stay?" and "What might tempt you to leave?"

When should you do them? Ideally, conduct stay interviews once a year or once every six months. And here's a secret: Don't wait for a scheduled time. If you sense someone is marching to a different beat, that's your trigger to schedule a stay interview with, say, Helen from accounting.

Who should initiate them? Usually the employee's direct supervisor, but it could be an HR representative or a coach; just ensure it's someone the employee trusts and feels comfortable opening up to.

Benefits of Stay Interviews:

- Early warning system: You catch issues before they become deal-breakers.

- Engagement booster: Employees feel valued when you ask for their input.

- Retention tool: By addressing concerns promptly, you keep your top talent from jumping ship.

- Culture thermometer: These interviews give you a real-time read on your company culture.

- Limitations of Stay Interviews:

- Time-consuming: Doing these regularly for every employee can eat up a lot of time.

- Skill-dependent: The effectiveness hinges on the interviewer's ability to ask the right questions and truly listen.

- Action required: If you ask for feedback and don't act on it, you might do more harm than good.

2. Exit Interviews

Now, let's flip the script and talk about exit interviews. These are the kinds of conversations you have when an employee is already on the way out, trying to figure out how the relationship went wrong after the breakup.

What are exit interviews? They're structured discussions with departing employees to understand their reasons for leaving and to gather feedback about their experience with the organization.

When to implement them? Ideally, conduct these in the employee's final week or two. You want them to have mentally checked out enough to be honest, but not so far gone that they don't care anymore.

Who should conduct them? Usually, HR representatives or third-party consultants and coaches. The goal is to create an environment where the departing employee feels safe to share honest feedback.

Benefits of Exit Interviews:

- Unfiltered feedback: Departing employees often feel freer to share their true thoughts.

- Insight gold mine: You get valuable information about what's working and what's not in your organization.

- Trend identification: Over time, you can spot patterns in why people leave.

- Closure: It provides a formal end to the employment relationship for both parties.

Limitations of Exit Interviews:

- Too little, too late: The insights you gain can't help retain the employee who's leaving.

- Emotion factor: Departing employees might be too angry or too checked out to provide constructive feedback.

- Sample bias: You only hear from those who are leaving, not those who stay.

The Big Difference

Stay interviews are forward-thinking and anticipatory, focused on the future, while exit interviews are retrospective and backward-looking, focused on the past. It's a subtle distinction, but it's easy to liken it to the difference between preventive medicine and an autopsy. Both have their uses, but only one helps you avoid problems to begin with.

Implementation Tips

1. Consistency is key: Develop a standard set of questions for both types of interviews. This allows you to compare responses over time and across departments.

2. Train your interviewers: Whether it's a stay or exit interview, the person conducting it needs excellent listening skills and the ability to dig deeper without making the employee feel interrogated.

3. Confidentiality is crucial: Employees need to trust that their honest feedback won't be used against them or shared inappropriately.

4. Act on the feedback: There's nothing more demoralizing than sharing your thoughts and seeing them ignored. Make sure you have a system in place to analyze and act on the insights you gain.

5. Mix it up: Consider using a combination of formats—face-to-face interviews, written surveys, and even anonymous feedback channels.

CONCLUSION

The Future of Performance Coaching and Its Impact on Organizations

As organizations continue to navigate a rapidly changing business environment, I am convinced that the importance of performance coaching will only continue to grow. I want to share a little about what's been keeping me up at night recently (in a good way, I promise!): the future of performance coaching. I've been one of the lucky ones, lasting long enough as a performance coach to see the evolution of the discipline for the past twenty years, and I am even more excited to think about all the changes that are still yet to come.

Lately, an increasing amount of my exchanges with corporate leaders has been on the topic of employee well-being. Organizations are slowly understanding the relationship between employee well-being and performance enhancement and engagement. As such, it's rather likely that future coaching programs will not only need to focus on traditional performance goals, but also integrate support for mental, emotional, and physical well-being. This ensures a more comprehensive approach to employee development, promoting overall health and job satisfaction.

And there's no doubt that technology is also transforming the coaching landscape. Technology is increasing the effectiveness and accessibility of modern-day coaching programs. Think virtual coaching platforms, AI-driven coaching tools, and data analytics. With all that at hand, organizations can personalize the process and thus offer a more tailored coaching experience while making it easier to track progress in real time.

At the same time, there is a growing emphasis on the critical value contributed by diversity and inclusion. Coaching will play a crucial role in addressing biases, as well as in developing inclusive leadership and supporting diverse talent. By prioritizing D&I, future coaching programs will help create more inclusive and equitable workplaces, fostering a culture of respect and collaboration.

As hybrid work models become increasingly prevalent, due to cost efficiencies and the geographical dispersion of our collaborators, coaching programs must adapt to support employees working in diverse environments. Effective performance coaching will need to address the unique challenges of remote and hybrid work by fostering connection, collaboration, and productivity despite physical distances. Organizations need to become more adaptable to ensure that all employees receive the support they need to succeed, regardless of their work setting.

An effective measurement of the impact of coaching programs will only be possible if organizations accept the increasing importance of data-driven decision-making. They will rely on data to assess coaching effectiveness and make informed decisions. Advanced analytics will provide deeper insights, helping organizations refine their approaches and achieve better outcomes. This reliance on data ensures that coaching remains relevant and impactful.

A holistic approach to development will also be a key differentiator among future coaching programs. Performance coaching will need to go beyond its initial performance focus and integrate a broad range of skills and competencies. As coaches, we will have to provide support to our employees to enhance their emotional intelligence, resilience, adaptability, and digital literacy. In this way, we can ensure that employees are well equipped to thrive in a dynamic business environment, fostering continuous personal and professional growth.

Finally, sustainable performance will be a key priority. Organizations will promote a balance between high performance and well-being, focusing on long-term development. Coaching programs will help employees build sustainable habits and avoid burnout. They will be promoting a culture that values both achievement and personal health. This is how organizations ensure that employees remain engaged and productive over the long-term, contributing to the overall success of the organization.

Final Thoughts and Advice for Leaders, HR Professionals, and Coaches

That's the part where I, once again, have to revert to my other hat. The academic one. And therefore, I have to be a bit more directive in regard to the work that still needs done. Performance coaching is without a doubt a potent source of individual and organizational success. And, as business leaders, HR professionals, and coaches, it's essential for us to stay informed about what's happening in, and with, the discipline. But we also need to clearly understand the evolving needs of our workforce. Consider the following few recommendations if you are set on maximizing the impact of your coaching programs.

Stay committed to continuous learning, and keep yourself updated on the latest research, trends, and best practices in performance coaching. Engage in professional-development opportunities. Attend conferences. Participate in industry networks. Talk to other coaches and peers within your industry. Without this necessary commitment, how can you ensure that your coaching strategies remain relevant and effective?

Next, foster a strong coaching culture within your organization, as it supports continuous learning and development, and leads to sustained organizational growth. Encourage your leaders to model coaching behaviors and provide your employees with opportunities for peer coaching and mentoring. This environment promotes the adoption of coaching principles throughout the organization, enhancing overall performance.

Enhance the effectiveness and accessibility of your coaching programs with technology. Offer personalized coaching experiences and measure their impact accurately via virtual coaching platforms, performance-tracking tools, and data analytics. Technology enables you to streamline coaching processes and provide more comprehensive support to your employees.

Prioritize diversity and inclusion in your coaching programs. Address biases, develop inclusive leadership, and support diverse talent to create a more equitable workplace. This focus will help build a culture of respect and collaboration. Enhance your overall organizational culture and promote diversity at all levels by ensuring that your coaching programs are inclusive and equitable.

Be adaptive and responsive to the shifting needs of your workforce. Adjust your coaching strategies to support employees in various environments and address their unique challenges. Your approach needs to be flexible to ensure that coaching remains effective regardless of the work setting.

Regularly measure and improve your coaching programs using both quantitative and qualitative metrics. Ensure that they remain effective and relevant by making informed improvements based on feedback gathered from participants and stakeholders. Refine them as often as necessary to guarantee that they are meeting the desired business outcomes and evolving as needed.

Acknowledge the relationship between employee well-being and performance to create a supportive environment where employees can thrive. Revise coaching programs to make your organization a healthier and more productive work environment by providing employees with resources and support for mental, emotional, and physical health.

Make holistic development a central component of your performance-development initiatives. Support your employees in their developmental journey to build emotional intelligence, resilience, adaptability, and other critical skills and competencies, as they are essential for thriving in a dynamic business environment. This will prepare them for various challenges and contribute to their long-term success.

Finally, I'll leave you here. Leaders, HR professionals, and coaches: I invite you to embrace the recommendations and insights set forth in this book to implement effective coaching programs that drive meaningful improvements among your employees, teams, and organizations. Performance coaching is a journey of continuous growth and development, and through coaching, you have the power to change the lives of all you encounter professionally—and, inevitably, transform your own.

www.ingramcontent.com/pod-product-compliance
Lightning Source LLC
LaVergne TN
LVHW041928070526
838199LV00051BA/2742